Evaluating the impact of your library

Evaluating the impact of your library

Sharon Markless
and
David Streatfield

facet publishing

Published by
Facet Publishing
7 Ridgmount Street
London WC1E 7AE

Facet Publishing is wholly owned by CILIP: the Chartered Institute of Library and Information Professionals.

First published 2006

British Library Cataloguing in Publication Data
A catalogue record for this book is available from the British Library.

ISBN-13: 978-1-85604-488-2
ISBN-10: 1-85604-488-2

Typeset in 10/13pt Revival 565 and Zurich by Facet Publishing.
Printed and made in Great Britain by MPG Books Ltd, Bodmin, Cornwall.

To the memory of

Harry Freedman, who would have taken great pride in
showing everyone his daughter's name on the front of this book,
regardless of the content

Doris and Bertram Blissett, parents of David Streatfield

Contents

Introduction

This book explores a major issue for library and information service managers of all kinds – evaluating the impact of services. Impact evaluation (or, as it is sometimes called, outcomes-based evaluation) has recently taken on new importance. All types of libraries and information services traditionally collect a range of performance information that can tell you as managers something about the *efficiency* of your services – sometimes flippantly described as 'busy-ness statistics'. What is now required is better information about the *effectiveness* of services, or the impact of services on users, including remote users.

Library and information service managers find it hard to get a grip on the slippery concept of service impact and many have struggled when trying to address impact questions in their planning. Now help is at hand. With the aid of UK national research funding, and with active support from professional bodies in the field, we have developed and tested an approach to evaluating impact that has helped managers in public, education, health and special libraries and information services. This book introduces our analysis of the issues and our approach to assessing service impact. The approach is designed to help you to understand, construct and deploy impact indicators that relate closely to what you are trying to achieve. The core chapters will take you through our rigorously tested process model for impact evaluation, with tools and examples to equip you with all that you need in order to address your own service impact questions.

You will find additional tools and materials linked to this book at www.facetpublishing. co.uk/evaluatingimpact.

We intend this to be a practical book designed to help busy managers to get to grips with impact issues. Therefore, although it is customary when writing books for professional library audiences to adopt an 'academic' tone, we have chosen instead to use the active voice and present tense where possible.

Sharon Markless and David Streatfield

Impact and all that:
use of some key terms in this book

The language of performance measurement is overstuffed with complex terms that are often used inconsistently even within the same book. Readers have probably come across all the expressions listed below when working on performance measurement. We try to show here how these terms interrelate, how they are used in this book and where impact fits into the overall picture.

Achievement

The term 'achievement' often crops up in the education world in relation to the impact of curriculum interventions or student learning support, to denote attaining a level of performance by effort. This term can overlap with 'impact', but it is unlikely that any library-based intervention or service will entirely account for an individual's 'achievement'. 'Achievement' is also used more technically in education circles to describe performance in a standardized test.

Aims and objectives

It doesn't take long to find inconsistencies in the use of the terms 'aims and objectives'. They are sometimes used interchangeably, even in the evaluation literature. When they are differentiated, people may talk about overarching aims and more specific objectives, but they may also talk about overarching objectives and precise aims. In the interests of sanity (ours and yours!) we define these terms for this book as:

aims – the main and overarching stated purposes of the library service or of the organization of which it is part
objectives – refinement of the aims into more specifically achievable terms, usually expressed as what can be achieved within one, three or (at most) five years.

Assessment *versus* evaluation

US writers on performance tend to use the terms 'assessment' and 'evaluation' as interchangeable. We prefer to use 'assessment' to describe judging people's knowledge or skills (and especially their educational performance); 'evaluation' is used here to refer to judging systems and services.

Effectiveness *versus* efficiency

It is slightly over-simple to say that traditional performance indicators as used by libraries (such as counting loans or occupancy rates) are focused on efficiency and that impact evaluation is concerned with effectiveness. However, this may be a useful distinction to bear in mind, since most library indicators tell us little or nothing about the effects of the services that are being measured or how these are perceived by users.

Evaluation *see* Assessment

Evidence

Evidence is any information or data that are used to answer a question (Carr, 1961). An important point made by Knight (2003) is that evidence is not a special category of information. It is information or data that people select to help them answer questions. As Knight says: 'One person's evidence is another's information.'

Impact

We define impact as any effect of the service (or of an event or initiative) on an individual or group. This effect may:

- be positive or negative
- be intended or accidental
- affect library staff, senior managers, users/customers, pupils, teachers, parents et al.

The impact can show itself in individual cases or through more generally discernible changes, such as shifts in:

- **quality of life**: e.g. self-esteem; confidence; feeling included; work or social prospects
- **educational and other outcomes**: e.g. skills acquired; educational attainment; levels of knowledge.

Impact evaluation

Evaluating impact using qualitative methods.

Impact measurement

Evaluating impact using quantitative methods (numbers). Some good work has been done using this approach, but it is important to remember that quantitative approaches tend to encourage us to focus on providing more to a larger number of people, and on faster or more efficient provision – in other words, unless we are careful they can lead us to concentrate on outputs not *outcomes* (q.v.).

Input, process, output model

This is the model that most people think of when they discuss performance indicators and the one that is most commonly used in libraries of all kinds. The three key elements of this model (as defined by Wavell et al., 2002) are:

Inputs – the resources the service requires in order to function (e.g. buildings, raw materials, staff and information)

Processes – what is done with the inputs; this may involve all sections of the service (e.g. preparing books for loan; cataloguing the collection; preparing an exhibition, educational programme or website; developing partnerships)

Outputs – the direct result on the service of combining inputs and processes. Outputs provide a measure of efficiency and are traditionally measured quantitatively (e.g. number of services provided and number of people provided for; numbers of books issued; proportion of the adult population attending learning sessions; numbers of visitors to an exhibition; number of reference enquiries answered). Output indicators are sometimes called service indicators.

The *input, process, output model* originated as an engineering process model. On the whole, this model has survived very well when transferred to other work contexts such as library service management. However, the analogy with the engineering system begins to break down when we start to look beyond outputs. When engineers are producing things and want to look at the overall effects of the process model, they usually do this by totalling up the outputs into 'direct outcomes'. This works well if the process involves, for example, manufacturing computers. If you bring together enough raw materials (inputs) and assemble them on a production line (processes) into working computers (outputs) the number produced is a good indication of the outcome. However, doing the same thing in the library world will not usually tell you anything about the overall effect – or impact.

Laws of impact evaluation

At various points in the book we have offered general points to guide people through the evaluation quagmire, in the form of 'laws of impact evaluation'. These 'laws' are all based on our practical experience of facilitating evaluation workshops involving over 700 library-service managers so far. Unlike real world laws, they should only be applied if you find them to be helpful.

Libraries (and information services)

This book is intended to help managers of libraries of all kinds. It should also be useful to providers of personal enquiry-based information services, that is, information services that engage with individual enquirers face-to-face, by telephone or by electronic means. The common factor here is that the services provided are intended to have a positive impact on the people served. Rather than employ the ugly acronym LIS in what follows, we have resorted to using 'libraries' in a generic sense in order to avoid constant repetition of 'libraries of all kinds and information services'. We apologize to any information-service managers who find this shorthand irksome. Where the focus is on particular kinds of libraries or specifically on information services we have tried to make this clear in the text.

Objectives *see* Aims

Outcomes

In the library context, outcomes can be thought of as the consequences of deploying services on the people who encounter them or on the communities served. These outcomes can be those intended or can be different from what was envisaged (unintended outcomes). A distinction is sometimes made between 'direct outcomes' (which are arrived at by aggregating outputs) and what people in the performance-measurement business describe as 'higher order' or 'longer term' outcomes. Outcomes of both kinds are not always clearly identifiable and they are often confused with outputs, even in the specialist literature. For this reason we prefer to use a more distinct generic term – *impact*.

Outputs *see* Input, process, output model

Performance indicators

A performance indicator (PI) is a statement against which achievement in an area of activity can be evaluated. It focuses on a *significant* feature of a system or service, enabling managers to monitor and evaluate the 'health' of the whole system or service (for example, many economists regard the level of unemployment as a reliable indicator of a national economic system). A range of performance indicators is needed to evaluate complex services such as libraries.

Performance indicators should provide at least one of the following:

- information about the performance of a system
- information about the central features of a system
- information on potential or existing problem areas

- information that is policy relevant
- information that can be compared with a previous or future time period.

Performance indicators are relatively stable – they usually change only if there are major changes in the aims and direction of the service or in how services are delivered. However, we should be more willing to consider changing our performance indicators, because they are usually difficult to get right first time and take time to develop. Gray and Wilcox (1995) described PIs as 'socially constructed abstractions arising from attempts to make sense of complex reality'.

Processes *see* Input, process, output model

Success criteria

In this book we refer to qualitative impact criteria as 'success criteria'. Choosing success criteria is the step required before deciding on your impact indicators. Success criteria should answer the questions: 'How can we tell if we are making a difference?' or 'How can we know that we are getting to where we want to be?' If you start off by identifying a series of criteria by which the service might be judged, you will end up with a list of specific qualitative statements (e.g. 'links into the local community'; 'equality of access to resources'). These then form the basis for creating indicators, which are assessable and may be quantifiable. As we will explain later, it is important to start with the judgement criteria rather than with the indicators themselves.

Targets

Targets are the short- or medium-term objectives for a service or activity expressed in terms of the chosen performance indicators. They may be thought of as performance indicators with numbers attached:

- Process targets usually focus on whether pre-specified changes (in what services are offered and how) are actually achieved within a set time period.
- Output targets are often fairly arbitrary and based on recent history (such as the previous year's output level). Such targets look for a specified change over the next time period. More sophisticated output targets take some account of changes in the environment in which services are offered as well as in the resources available to provide them.
- Impact targets are posed in terms of what level of difference the service should make (to the community, to individuals and groups, or to organizations involved). They are focused on what the service has achieved.

Unlike performance indicators, which are relatively stable, targets change as the service moves on.

Process and output targets are usually generated by and fit into the annual planning cycle of your organization. However, impact targets may not naturally fit into the planning year. As one service manager said:

> The trouble with government indicators is that they are all geared to the annual financial cycle. Impact does not occur to fit the annual cycle and has to be viewed over a longer term.

These definitions are offered for use in this book. However, the literature on managing change emphasizes how important it is to use the accepted local vocabulary when you are working with your colleagues. It may be better to put up with a bit of sloppy language when precision isn't vital than to distance yourself from other people by insisting on using your own preferred terms (or ours).

Part 1
The context

1

The demand for evidence

If you are interested in the impact of your library services, or of library services in general, you may like to start by reflecting on where the impetus towards impact evaluation is coming from and how that impetus can itself distort the picture. These issues are explored below. However, if your concerns are purely practical please go on to Chapter 4.

1.1 Why is evidence of impact an issue for libraries (and information services)?[1]

Picture a group of scholars working in the Library of Alexandria in about 50 BC. Now assume that they have been ferried forward in time and deposited in your library today. Will they identify their surroundings as a library? More specifically, will the scholars recognize the printed publications at the heart of your library as equivalent in some way to their scrolls? If so, it seems likely that they will know their surroundings as a library. But what happens if we ship them forward another 30 years and touch them down again? Will your library still be there? Will it be recognizable as a library? Will information technology and the demand for different kinds of interaction between library staff, users and the service have transformed the library beyond recognition?

Even the most sensitive crystal ball is unlikely to offer a clear picture of libraries 30 years hence because of the accelerating rate of change. However, if we can start to gauge the changes in the impact of various services, this will give us an indication of where things are going and help in managing the changes needed to get there.

We don't have to look 30 years ahead to make a case for looking at impact. One common feature of all types of libraries is that there is too much to do and too little time. 'Traditional' performance indicators are important for enabling you to tell whether aspects of a service are working efficiently. However, when a new initiative or project is undertaken, this is usually achieved by prising precious time away from other operational activities. If this is the case, it is doubly important to know whether the innovation is working and how. More specifically, are you using this precious time well? How can your innovation be made to work better? Are there lessons from your current initiatives or projects that have implications for how you deliver the rest of the service? Do you need to know more about them? Asking these sorts of questions should move you towards gathering impact evidence that will tell you whether you are working along the right lines or whether you should be doing different things in different ways.

What are the big factors to be taken into account when evaluating the impact of innovations and the effects of accelerating organizational change? The most immediately obvious and pervasive influence is the accelerating expansion in information and communications technologies. These advances are raising a plethora of questions about library services provision, all of which demand impact evidence if sensible answers are to be adopted. Some of these changes and the questions they raise are reviewed below.

1.1.1 The impact of ICT

Advances in information technology are already making huge differences to the range of services offered by libraries, the expectations of library users and the roles of library staff. We offer some examples of change in libraries below followed by some questions in italic. If libraries are to make real advances in the 'Age of Information' they need to be able to answer many of these questions.

1 Libraries now have much **more information available** to them electronically than even five years ago, some of which could not have been realistically provided without enormous advances in computer power. Some of this information is only available on subscription and some of it is also available in traditional published form, raising a variety of questions.

   • *How much should the library spend on traditional forms of publication as against e-publications and electronic information?*
   • *Do different users (e.g. students seeking information, scholars, recreational readers, people with visual impairment) prefer traditional forms of publication or electronic access?*
   • *Should libraries subscribe to a wider range of electronic publications and, if so, which ones?*
   • *On what basis should they review and update these decisions?*
   • *Should collections and services be managed locally or remotely, licensed for a fee or freely available?*

2 Since the internet (or 'surface web') offers more or less ready access to vast amounts of current or dated information, misinformation and disinformation, most of which cannot readily be filtered by libraries (see paragraph 3), this puts a premium on a range of **information literacy skills** that users may or may not have acquired. Users need to be able to select and reject information for a purpose, to identify and take account of biased information, and to decide whether information from a particular source can be seen as authoritative.

   • *What is the role for library staff, if any, in helping people to acquire and develop appropriate information literacy skills?*
   • *How should they interact with other people, such as teachers, who have a role in information literacy development?*

- *Do different types of libraries (e.g. health, education or public libraries) have different roles in information literacy development?*

3 Library staff should be better equipped than the average library user to **identify high quality information on the internet**, they may have more time to do so and if they adopt a guidance role they may be able to steer users towards the most appropriate sources (whether these are electronic or traditional publications).

- *Is the way forward for library staff to be proactive in creating websites and multimedia web pages to promote library services and give easier access to various information sources?*
- *Should they go further and seek to set up gateways through which users can identify and gain access to selected, good quality information sources (helping to construct the 'deep web')?* [2]

4 Libraries of all kinds are increasingly **investing in computer technology** and are reorganizing available space to accommodate this change. Public libraries offer an alternative means for people, and especially less affluent people, to gain access to the internet.

- *Since libraries are not the only potential providers of access to information (alternatives include computer services or basic skills units in education, internet cafés or specialist information centres for the general public) to what extent should libraries become computer providers?*
- *What effect will increased public access to the internet from home have on library-based internet provision?*

5 It is widely predicted that developments in information and communications technologies (ICTs) will have great impact on **key areas of library work**, notably:

— reader development
— access by potential service users
— information provision
— supporting lifelong learning (including information literacy)
— social inclusion – attracting users from sectors of society that have not traditionally been heavy library users.

- *How can information technologies be harnessed to actively encourage people to read more widely and deeply?*
- *Can doors be opened to potential readers who are attracted by ICT?*
- *How can library access best be enhanced using ICT?*
- *How can libraries establish their place in the pantheon of electronic information providers and how high a priority should this be?*

- *How can ICT be deployed to engage with a wider range of potential library users and which should be the priority groups to target?*
- *If libraries become successful in attracting new groups of users, what will be the effect on the existing core users?*

All of these questions are regularly raised by library managers in our workshops focused on evaluating the impact of library services. They usually have the same effect on participants – rather like hitting a brick wall. What rapidly becomes clear is that the traditional performance data collected by most libraries will not help to generate answers to these questions; nor do they equip staff to make operational or strategic decisions in these areas. Most library statistics still concentrate on monitoring the efficiency of the services currently being offered rather than their impact on users. Library managers usually do not have enough evidence of the impact of their current services to be able to tell how well they are doing, let alone having enough evidence to gauge whether a particular new service or intervention is likely to work. Fortunately, we have found ways of addressing these issues, which we will describe in later chapters.

1.1.2   The pressure to evaluate impact

Moving towards the electronic library may be bringing about a transformation in library-staff roles, user expectations, service delivery methods and visions of access, but this is only part of the change agenda. As Denise Troll Covey (2002) observed when commenting on the US academic library scene:

> Governments and institutions are clamouring for accountability. In a marketplace penetrated by technology and free and easy access to information on the 'surface Web' (information of dubious quality for the purposes of higher education), academic libraries must compete for the attention of users or potential users, advertise their resources available on the 'deep Web', and somehow measure their impact on the learning and research outcomes of their institution.

But what other factors are fuelling the drive towards impact evidence-gathering? Three of the obvious pressure points might be labelled 'the accountability obsession', 'the value for money drive' and 'the evidence-based working aspiration'. These are more fully outlined below.

1.1.3   A growing focus on performance management and accountability in public institutions

The idea of evaluating performance is not new, but it is more heavily embedded in some areas of work than in others. To take the most obvious example, assessment of student performance is heavily rooted in *national education systems* at all levels through internal tests, external examinations and, in many countries, through standardized assessment at various ages in schools. Inspection frameworks, for schools through to universities, now require more rigorous collection of evidence as well as the demonstration of analytical judgements based on this evidence. At the same time, national and federal governments are trying to create more consistent institutional management by demanding that all education institutions produce development plans addressing prescribed issues. There is also a growing movement towards evaluating the quality of teaching and of looking more broadly at the student experience within the education system.

The demand for more and better evidence of service efficiency and effectiveness has rapidly extended into other public service areas and is increasingly being felt in libraries of all kinds. The strength and focus of library target setting, benchmarking and efforts at standardization of services varies from country to country, but the trend towards greater accountability appears inexorable.

In this era of increased advocacy of public service accountability by national and local politicians, library managers have to be visibly on top of the evidence – this means not only collecting information but also being seen to analyse, interpret and apply the evidence with the (ostensible) aim of improving library services. How much real improvement results from all this activity will depend upon larger political factors such as the strength of the organizational will to bring about change, but a key contributory element is likely to be how much the evidence collected and analysed tells library managers about the impact of their current services and innovations.

In the UK, public library services were until recently required to submit annual library plans to central government and they are also subjected to government-imposed service reviews, various benchmarking and standards initiatives, and the introduction of national standards and impact measures.

The UK National Health Service is preoccupied with accountability and is heavily target-driven. In particular, the mantra invoked when looking at any aspect of the health service is that it should have 'a positive impact on the quality of patient care'. It is sometimes hard to find evidence to demonstrate how this aim can be met by developing library services!

1.1.4   The value for money ethos

The policy concern with public accountability is closely linked to a focus on perceived service effectiveness – but a view of effectiveness that tends to be narrowly defined in cost-benefit terms – getting more for less money. Public services are widely viewed by politicians as requiring constant rationing and reduction, although they usually prefer to talk about 'cutting out waste' rather than admitting that they want to reduce or remove highly regarded services such as libraries.

Within the organization a narrowly finance-driven approach may create a managerial environment in which it is necessary to argue for funding based on 'results'. In this kind of environment the 'results' will again tend to be narrowly defined in terms of increased use or happier users (or, in higher education, increased levels of student retention), rather than what benefits people get from the services or whether different approaches might be more effective.

1.1.5 Rediscovering information

Until relatively recently, the processes involved in managing information in organizations were largely taken for granted. Although Henry Mintzberg (1973) identified three generic information roles among the ten that he attributed to all managers three decades ago, the idea that information should be managed alongside the traditional activities of managing people, finance and material resources was slow to take root.

Again, from the late 1970s onwards, advances in information technology played an important part here. With the advent of affordable mainframe computers and later of networked personal computers, proposals to spend substantial sums of money on efficient organization of various types of information, which had previously been handled less efficiently as an invisible part of various people's jobs, tended to bring these information areas into sharper focus.

In the 1980s, the process of promoting information up organizational agendas was greatly assisted by Michael Porter (1985), who advanced the idea that better information is what brings organizational success. Porter's version of *competitive advantage*, based on the 'value chain' (fed by strategic information) in turn led to other information-centred formulations such as the 'learning company', knowledge management and 'evidence-based policy and practice'.

How far have these ideas penetrated into the core of library and information management thinking? The idea of competitive advantage gave business information services a powerful advocacy tool and some library service managers have made efforts to reconstitute themselves as higher status knowledge managers. However, by no means all library services have reached the point where they feel the need to introduce, for example, a strategic information strategy (as distinct from an information technology implementation and training plan).

1.1.6 Towards evidence-based library and information work

The idea of *evidence-based policy and practice* (EBPP) is potentially more important for the library and information service world, if only because it has taken organizational root in some traditionally strong areas of library service provision, notably health. The core idea emerged in the medical world in Canada and the USA as 'evidence-based health care' and was rapidly transplanted to Australasia and the UK (see Muir Gray, 1997), before being taken up in the education and social care sectors and by some national governments. In essence, EBPP is about systematic collection and interpretation of valid, important and applicable evidence.

It is clear that EBPP is interpreted in somewhat different ways in the various sectors involved. For example, in the UK health sector there is a strong focus on meta-clinical evidence as a guide to decision-making, but a growing recognition that different evidence rules apply at the public health end of the continuum; in social care and in education the focus is very much on the nature of acceptable evidence, while the UK Government emphasis is primarily on securing a range of evidence to help in the formation, implementation and evaluation of policy. However, all these approaches recognize that the policy and practice evidence base draws (more or less confidently) upon a variety of sources, including:

- academic research evidence
- practice-generated impact evidence
- professionally mediated 'best practice' information.

In other words, EBPP concerns are very much the concerns of this book.

When it comes to applying EBPP principles in practice, the key concerns common to all the main public sector applications (see Streatfield, 2003) include:

- availability of sufficient evidence of high enough quality to inform a specific practice question
- synthesis of the available evidence on a key question to provide an overview of the findings
- adequate dissemination of the evidence to enable practitioners to gain access to the evidence in an appropriate form
- identification of gaps in the evidence and strategic initiatives to fill important gaps
- disciplined reporting of the research processes and the evidence in 'practitioner-friendly' manner, to enable practitioners to gauge the relevance, importance and reliability of the evidence
- fostering of a strategic and operational management climate to encourage EBPP
- introduction of structures and mechanisms to encourage application of EBPP approaches
- professional development support for managers to equip them to find and appraise the evidence
- active debate about the nature and basis of professional knowledge and practice.

All of these components raise issues for evidence-based library work, but some progress has been made. Two of the leading advocates (Brice and Booth, 2004) recently asked and answered the key question:

Is it possible to adapt the evidence-based practice model to librarianship and information work? To do so involves applying the results from rigorous research studies to professional practice to improve the quality of services to users.

There is already a professional textbook in place (Booth and Brice, 2004) as well as an International Evidence-Based Librarianship Conference (heavily dominated by health librarians) and they have initiated a process of identifying and refining key research questions for the field. (See www.eblib.net.) At the heart of the process is a combination of user-reported, librarian-observed and research-derived evidence (Booth, 2002). Once this movement expands beyond the medical world (assuming that this is ever achieved) the whole process might be seen as providing a framework to exploit impact evidence systematically.

1.2   Emerging interest in the management of change

How much change are we really looking at? In her commentary on US academic libraries (2002), Covey observes that:

> Development of the digital library precipitates massive change, not only in delivery formats and access methods, but also in work and workflow, staffing, the scope of library instruction, and assessment efforts. . . . Web access and capabilities have brought with them the need for libraries to engage in the design, management, and assessment of multimedia Web pages, portals, and products. . . . Libraries are conducting surveys, focus groups, user protocols, transaction log analysis, and other kinds of research to assess traditional and digital resource use; the usability of online resources; user needs, expectations, and satisfaction; and the quality of library services and facilities. They are grappling with how to assess research and learning outcomes, cost-effectiveness, and cost-benefits.

These demands and challenges appear to be transforming all types of libraries. Specific drivers of change include substantial programmes of ICT implementation in libraries of all kinds (such as the People's Network national implementation and development programme for public libraries in the UK) and linked training initiatives aimed at equipping library staff to work in electronic environments (public library staff and school librarians have been targeted for central-government-driven initiatives in the UK).

If we take the levels of uptake of training workshops in various countries as an indicator of evolving professional development priorities among library staff it is clear that there is burgeoning demand for:

- ICT skills training focused on the changing work of library staff in e-information environments
- education and training focused on the roles of librarians as teachers and trainers
- more help in development planning as services adapt to the demands of increasingly ICT-based services.

The accompanying rhetoric is of transforming libraries and of the penalties if opportunities are missed to establish libraries centrally in the new information landscape. Interestingly, the People's Network has chosen to move beyond rhetoric in commissioning 'toolkits' linked to training programmes to help library service managers in grappling with the issues of managing change (www.mla.gov.uk/action/ pn/change.asp). One central message from this work is that serious attention to change involves gaining greater clarity about what sorts of change are desirable, what change is inevitable and about the effects of change – based on evidence about what works. In this sense, moving towards more effective management of change is leading to greater need for impact evidence.

1.3   What is distorting the picture?

It is obvious to anyone who looks at the issues of evaluating the impact of library services that this is not a problem-free and straightforward process. As we will show in the next chapter, impact is a slippery concept that many service managers find difficult to grasp. But the problems begin even before the individual library-service manager starts to get to grips with the concept. We have identified in this chapter some of the factors that are currently pushing libraries towards impact evaluation: the problem is that all of these factors can have a more or less profound distorting effect on how (and indeed, whether) we engage in gathering evidence of impact.

Taking these factors in roughly the order that they were introduced earlier, the gallop towards electronic libraries, the accountability obsession (and the value for money drive) and even the evidence-based working aspiration can all make life more difficult for the manager who wants to get a real hold on impact. There may also be problems with conflicting agendas and with our capacity to get involved seriously in gathering evidence of effectiveness.

1.3.1   Being realistic about evaluating ICT initiatives

We need to decide *when* collecting evidence is a good idea and *what* we are doing this for.

Staff of library services are racing to equip themselves as leading providers of access to the internet and to learn the new skills required to help their users to become confident users of electronic information sources. Unfortunately, the base from which many libraries are starting does not help. As David Murray (2003) noted:

> When we roll out a superb development – the People's Network for example – we graft it on to a failing infrastructure and hope the public will see 'new library'. Too often, what they see is a load of new computers and new furniture in a building that's coming apart at the seams.

Similarly, many libraries are making efforts to engage users with ICT but without sufficient computers or licensed software to take this on realistically. Their staff may be striving to help users but may not themselves have sufficient training or experience in effective internet searching, or in providing one-to-one tuition or small group training.

Impact, in this less than favourable context, is likely to mean 'any change in our users that may have come about despite the unsuitable environment, lack of confidence or competence in some staff and the depredations of years of systematic under-funding'. This may not be important, if the evaluation is being conducted primarily to inform managers about what needs to be addressed first, but there is a real issue about impact evidence-collection for other purposes.

Service evaluation is, among other things, a political process, especially if the intention is to use the evidence to secure funds or to account to politicians or senior organizational managers. You may want to evaluate services that are being delivered in heavily unfavourable conditions and present the case for change – if there is a real chance of changing those conditions. To do such an evaluation in less optimistic circumstances may simply provide evidence to be used by others to allocate blame – in your direction.

1.3.2   The obsession with accountability

In the 'value for money' organizational environment, securing a share of diminishing organizational funds may become a ritual dance with its own rules, which may or may not involve presentation of high-quality evidence of effectiveness. In such an environment, presenting impact evidence as part of the case for service development may be vital or it may be more important to go through the motions of doing so. Evidence-based decision-making may be a key to success in your organization but it may also be a notion to which strategic managers pay lip service.

Attention to the financial 'bottom line' is of course important for all organizations but, even in the private sector, there is growing concern that if we only think in narrow 'value for money' terms this may result in throwing out the creative and productive baby with the organizational bathwater. The concern does not end here. 'Called to account' was the theme of a recent prestigious lecture given to commemorate the founder-director of the British Broadcasting Corporation (BBC), in which Onora O'Neill (2002) observed:

> For those of us in the public sector the new accountability takes the form
> of detailed control. . . . The new accountability culture aims at ever more
> perfect administrative control of institutional and professional life.

But what happens in practice when this approach is applied (at least in the UK)? According to O'Neill:

> In the universities external examiners lost influence as centrally planned
> teaching quality assessment was imposed; in the health services professional
> judgement is constrained in many ways; in schools curriculum and assessment
> of pupils is controlled in pretty minute detail. Schools, hospitals and universities

are then all judged and funded by their rankings in league tables of performance indicators.

In theory the new culture of accountability and audit makes professionals and institutions more accountable to the public. This is supposedly done by publishing targets and levels of attainment in league tables, and by establishing complaint procedures by which members of the public can seek redress for any professional or institutional failures. But underlying this ostensible aim of accountability to the public the real requirements are for accountability to regulators, to departments of government, to funders, to legal standards. . . . Intelligent accountability, I suspect, requires more attention to good governance and fewer fantasies about total control.

What can we do to counter the tendency towards top-down control? Good governance, in the sense suggested by O'Neill, requires us to move on from arbitrary performance indicators that may corrupt the services they are intended to evaluate by concentrating effort in inappropriate areas. Instead, we need high-quality evidence-gathering about the effectiveness of library services, allied to sound professional judgements in interpreting the evidence and proposing appropriate action. The process model described in Part 2 of this book should help to achieve these goals.

One other disturbing tendency that we have noted is for government departments and their national or local agencies to blur the important distinction between evaluating innovative programmes and making the advocacy case to do more of the same. Evaluation of initiatives should help to show what is working more or less well, which elements in the programme need remedial attention or should be more widely adopted, and whether the initiative represents good value for money. If the 'evaluation' assumes the last point and concentrates on showing how everything in the garden is lovely, this ceases to be evaluation and is not a good foundation on which to build a convincing case for development.

The fantasies about total control are not confined to the public sector. Looking at the world of business, Kaplan and Norton (1992) noted:

because traditional measurement systems have sprung from the finance function, the systems have a control bias. That is, traditional performance measurement systems specify the particular actions they want employees to take and then measure to see whether the employees have in fact taken those actions. In that way, the systems try to control behaviour. Such measurement systems fit with the engineering mentality of the Industrial Age.

How should the business world set about performance measurement in the Post-industrial Age? Their solution is 'the balanced scorecard', which

. . . puts strategy and vision, not control, at the centre. It establishes goals but assumes that people will adopt whatever behaviour and take whatever actions are necessary to arrive at those goals.

We will return to the balanced scorecard in section 3.1 and explore its usefulness in selecting appropriate impact indicators across four important perspectives.

Best Value Reviews involving UK Public libraries

One strand of national accountability introduced into UK local government in recent years is the Best Value Review framework. The strong implication of introducing Best Value Review programmes into local government is that if services cannot be shown to be robust and responsive to real demand they should close. Library service managers need to be able to answer fundamental questions such as 'Can this service be better delivered in other ways?' or 'Is our reading promotion campaign having any real effect?'

A significant danger in applying the Review framework is that services are actively encouraged to base their decision-making on evidence derived from consultation with users and potential users of services. Since the framework does not distinctly identify a role for local experts (in this case library-service managers) alongside the opinions of the general public, the Review process can result in professional judgement being marginalized or ignored when services are changed.

Since there are always cheaper ways of doing anything, this may distort the Best Value intentions about effective provision – unless evidence of impact can be gathered to demonstrate 'added value'.

The Best Value Review process entails considering your service from four angles – challenge (yourselves), consult, compare and compete – known as the four Cs. Our review process is seen to help. According to participants in one of the project workshops:

This process helps in relation to all four 'Cs':
Challenge: Do customers agree (consult) that these are the priorities/objectives? Do the services deliver against these objectives?
Consult: Asking customers whether the objectives are being met.
Compare: How are other services (of any kind – compete) faring in relation to these objectives? How are other services delivering against these objectives?
Compete: We need to consider the medium-term threat of internet providers.

1.3.3 Is evidence-based working the answer?

When Mahatma Gandhi was asked by an interviewer what he thought about Western civilization he answered 'I think it would be a good idea'. Evidence-based policy and practice (EBPP) probably falls into the same category, at least for the immediate future. However, the idea of EBPP is already under challenge.

The contention that basing decisions on evidence (or aspiring to do so) is not enough has been well articulated by Peter Knight (2003). He asserts unequivocally that 'Evidence cannot prescribe action' and that 'It is more fruitful to think about expertise-based practice in complex settings' before observing that 'evidence' is only as good as the questions we ask and calling on higher education researchers to learn to ask better questions. He then navigates into the long-running debate about the relationship (if any) between research evidence and policy decision-making, arguing that 'evidence' needs to be *mediated*, because it is complicated, *complemented* because it is incomplete, and *championed* because even strong evidence gets ignored otherwise. Finally, he calls for expertise-based, rather than evidence-based, policy and practice. 'Experts', he says, 'are plainly informed by evidence but they add value to it, by making judgements about cases not directly covered by the evidence at hand and identifying areas in need of study.' They can also, he hopes, 'engage with policy-makers in ways that inert evidence cannot'.

Following on from Knight's arguments we suggest that the appropriate aspiration is towards *expertise-based and evidence-informed decision making.* (It is interesting to note that the main UK centre for EBPP in education[3] prefers to talk about evidence-informed rather than evidence-based practice.)

1.3.4   Beware of 'methodological fundamentalism'

There is a further problem with evidence-based working, if too narrow a definition of evidence is adopted. The information research community in the USA is increasingly recognizing that, to have any real recognition by policy makers and government funders, it is necessary for them to venture out into the surrounding educational research territory.

The problem is, that for the research to be taken seriously by the present Federal Government, it has to feature in a charming website called the What Works Clearinghouse (WWC),[4] established by the US Department of Education's Institute of Education Sciences. The criteria for inclusion within the Clearinghouse are, to say the least, rigid: the research reports submitted to their review process are classified in one of three categories:

* '**Meets evidence standards**' – randomized controlled trials and regression discontinuity designs that meet their specific criteria (virtually impossible to achieve in any real educational research project concerned with library or information service provision)
* '**Meets evidence standards with reservations**' – strong quasi-experimental studies that have comparison groups and meet their other evidence standards
* '**Does not meet evidence screens**' – studies that provide insufficient evidence of causality or otherwise fall foul of the WWC criteria.

The nasty trap for unwary researchers is that if you aspire to getting your research included in the second category and fail, you are then consigned to the 'Does not meet evidence screens' group. Not the most promising start to a postgraduate research career![5]

But it is not only the US Department of Education's Institute of Education Sciences that appears to have given way to what the leading educational researcher Ernest

House (2004) called 'methodological fundamentalism'. In a paper presented to the European Evaluation Society, he pointed to various fundamentalist trends in US Central Government, before claiming that:

> This authoritarian attitude has spread to other levels of [US] government. . . . Some government agencies demand that all evaluations must be randomized experiments. Other ways of producing evidence are not scientific and not acceptable. There is one method for discovering the truth and one method only – the randomized experiment. If we employ randomized experiments, they will lead us to a Golden Age in education and social services. Such is the revelatory vision. There are sacred figures from the past and sacred texts. Core believers are absolutely certain they are right, that randomized experiments reveal the truth. They do not listen to critics, and they do not comprehend the arguments against the method. A mandate for randomized trials has been written into legislation without discussion with professional communities. Avoiding contrary ideas is part of the orientation, and, of course, the policy is enforced by government edict.

1.3.5   Conflicting priorities

In some cases there may be conflict between the larger policy agenda and organizational priorities. For example, national policy makers may call on organizations to adopt an impact-focused and user-needs-centred approach but internal organizational pressures may dictate a more limited and less challenging outputs-focused approach. Where national policy includes setting targets for a whole sphere of work, such as schools or the health service, these may be so general that they cannot be readily translated into library-service contribution terms. We have already noted that health library services usually have only an indirect and diffuse impact on the quality of client care; similarly, although it is possible to show that schools that are equipped with good libraries tend to produce better exam results, it is much harder to show how anything done within a particular school library directly affects student examination performance.

We may also have conflicting priorities about where and how intensively to focus in relation to service impact within our own library service. Should we give attention to areas in which we can readily be shown to be failing, or concentrate on our main successes? Is it astute to focus, for example, on the relationships between academic staff and library staff in education settings or would this be counter-productive?

Since all libraries are short of time, and given that collecting impact evidence takes time and effort, what proportion of the performance evaluation for your library should be focused on impact? Will all the key players agree to spending the time required? There may also be concerns about timescales. Much of the evidence-gathering in organizations runs to an annual reporting cycle but looking at the impact of innovation in any significant area of work may well require a longer timescale. And how well attuned is your organization to the need to gather impact evidence at all? Will going down this road tend to isolate the library from the larger organization?

The key to answering these questions is to decide why you are looking for evidence of impact. If you are doing this primarily to account to the parent organization or to secure additional funding, it is important to choose ways of gathering evidence that will accord to the predominant organizational ethos. If you are gathering evidence to meet external project-funding requirements then it is likely that the parameters will be set as part of the contract award process. On the other hand, if you are focusing on impact primarily to inform yourselves as managers so that you can improve the service, then any evidence that you will find convincing is acceptable.

1.3.6   Are we ready for the challenge?

Gathering evidence of impact may be highly desirable but how well are library service managers equipped to take on this work? The US academic library survey (Covey, 2002) quoted earlier asked how well service managers felt they were doing and where the problems emerge. They reported that:

> Current evaluation efforts are often inefficient and ineffective because of inadequate skills, poor planning, cumbersome governance, and a fundamental frame of reference ill-suited to evaluation.

Around data gathering there was concern that:

- the most readily available data might not be the most valuable
- valuable time is spent gathering useless data
- useful data are not applied to full advantage if at all.

Other issues identified were:

> Being at the mercy of commercial vendors and software developers who define and measure different user transactions differently. . . .
> . . . often the data gathered in library surveys, focus groups, think-aloud protocols, and other user studies are imprecise, difficult to analyse or interpret and turn out to be inappropriate to the research purpose. Even when meaningful data are gathered, they can languish without being used.
> . . . instances of data being difficult or impossible to analyse and interpret because the research instruments were poorly designed and inadequately tested. . . . focus groups moderators who could not effectively manage domineering participants or engage timid participants, or who had their own agenda or biases that drove the discussion. . . . user protocols undermined by librarians who could not refrain from answering the participants' questions and assisting them when they had trouble performing the protocol tasks.

Our process model is designed to deal with these kinds of issues.

1.4   Why is it important to tackle impact?

1.4.1   What is driving the change?

We have tried to show that there are a number of different drivers pushing organiz-ations towards evaluating their effectiveness. As we will see later, different approaches to evaluating impact and different types of evidence will be appropriate depending on whether the demand is coming from:

- the federal/national government level (characterized by very strategic and apparently simplistic targets that are prone to change at short notice)
- external inspection regimes focused on service improvement or the achievement of standards
- the institution of which the library service is part (requiring effectiveness priorities to accord with institutional targets)
- the managers of the library service (focusing on greater understanding of what makes services work well)
- the members of or participants in the service (where the motives for looking at impact may vary substantially).

It is also important to recognize that there are still many work areas where efficiency monitoring is all that is required; when for example:

- there is no pressure to show impact – there are few demands for evidence from inside or outside the organization
- it may not yet be politic to broadcast or share impact evidence (even if individual service managers choose to focus on impact as well as 'busy-ness statistics' to inform their own management decision-making)
- there is a tacit conspiracy *not* to look too closely at whether large sums of money are being spent well!

Curiously, one of the areas in which effective performance has not been taken seriously, until very recently, is the implementation of ICT programmes, unless counting 'hits' on a website can be assumed to be evaluating anything. Various surveys of ICT projects have found that there is usually no real attempt to evaluate them and that when any questions *are* asked they normally stop at the point of establishing whether the installation works, rather than going on to ask whether it could have been done better or was worth doing at all. This situation is now changing fairly rapidly, at least where there is more or less direct competition between traditional and new ways of providing services.

1.4.2   Why move on?

There are several reasons why library services should be giving more attention to impact evaluation:

External factors

- The political agenda is changing. The drive towards greater accountability may have a distorting effect on service provision – unless we can come up with good quality evidence about what works and how.
- There is a danger that externally imposed performance targets will be confined to evidence drawn from output measures and ignore much of what libraries are achieving.
- Being effective in meeting government priorities (for example regarding social inclusion, lifelong learning and parity of access) may require additional service expenditure. Success in addressing these issues will have to be demonstrated to justify this. Capacity building in communities requires good evidence.
- There are opportunities for libraries operating in different fields to learn from each other about how to demonstrate success effectively.

Internal factors

- Choosing targets carefully and gathering appropriate evidence is an important management skill – the process encourages clarity and helps to focus on priorities.
- Focusing on a limited number of aims and impact indicators should make you question why certain things are not happening. For example, why is the well staffed and stocked library not a first port of call for senior managers in this organization?
- Where impact targets are integrated into practice this should lead to higher staff motivation, because they can see what they want to achieve, why they are doing things and what success they are having ('this is more satisfying than just jumping through hoops').

1.4.3   What library managers say

We have looked briefly at why there is a growing demand for evidence of the impact of services and at how these pressures can distort the picture. But why do library service managers get involved in yet another time-consuming activity? The evidence from several hundred managers who have participated in our workshops is that they usually get involved for one or more of seven reasons (in descending order of frequency of mention):

- **Focus for development**. Most managers want to know whether they are being effective and what they need to do to get better.
- **Internal accountability**. Increasingly, parent organizations want to know not just whether their library services are working efficiently but how well they are contributing to the overall organizational goals.
- **External accountability**. We have already shown that national and federal governments are seeking greater accountability (or control) from public services. They may want to focus on service impact, but even if they resort to more traditional performance measures it may be important to focus on impact in order to show the full extent of the library contribution.

- **Professional pride/job satisfaction**. The demand for impact evidence from senior management or from government is not universal. Even where there are no external pressures, some managers want to get involved in looking at their service impact because they want to be sure that they are doing a good job – even if there is little scope for development.
- **Status/profile**. Although this may not be an incentive at the outset, many managers report that one of the benefits of undertaking impact evaluation is greater recognition or more positive feedback from their users. These effects can be quite specific (such as when various school librarians field tested school library self-evaluation materials that mirrored the school self-evaluation framework about to be introduced and were seen by teachers as 'instant experts' on self-evaluation because of this) but asking questions about your service is likely to produce answers – some of which will be encouraging!
- **Securing additional resources**. Where organizations are demanding impact evidence as part of the resource allocation process, it makes sense to get involved. In any case it will help your argument if you can show that you are being effective in ways that interest the fundholders.
- **Survival**. Libraries are no longer automatically seen as 'a good thing' and there is increasing competition from other 'support services', especially organizational computer services and the internet. Libraries are (relatively) expensive to provide – so why bother? Assembling good quality evidence of the impact of services currently being provided should help to fight off any future threat to libraries – if the threat is current it may be too late to start!

Notes

1   For our use of 'libraries' and 'information services' in the text please see 'Impact and all that: use of some key terms in this book' on page xiii.

2   Various groups of UK university libraries have collaborated to create subject-based gateways for different academic disciplines, with funding provided by the Joint Information Systems Committee (JISC; www.jisc.ac.uk). Examples include BUBL UK catalogue of internet resources (http://bubl.ac.uk); EEVL, the internet guide to engineering, mathematics and computing (www.eevl.ac.uk); the Humbul humanities hub (www.humbul.ac.uk); and SOSIG, the social science information gateway (www.sosig.ac.uk).

3   The Evidence for Policy and Practice Information (EPPI) Centre based at the University of London Institute of Education (http://eppi.ioe.ac.uk).

4   What Works Clearinghouse (www.w-w-c.org/).

5   This concern, and what to do about it, was a major theme of the *International Research Colloquium on School Libraries* organized by the Center for International Scholarship in School Libraries, Rutgers University, held in New York in April–May 2005. The research methods group at this event was led by Keith Curry Lance – the last comment is his.

2

Getting to grips with impact

If you have decided to do some impact evaluation, or to try out the process, you may want to go straight on to Chapter 4. If you are interested in some of the difficulties inherent in evaluating impact and in gathering and interpreting evidence read on.

2.1   A metaphor and a model

The language and underpinning concepts of performance measurement are often arcane and sometimes confusing. This is probably because the basic metaphor of performance indicators and targets and the associated vocabulary were developed by engineers when looking at system efficiency and appropriated by accountants to simplify and 'measure' the complex world of managing organizations.

It is hardly surprising that the concepts of performance measurement work reasonably well when the library is considered as a more or less efficient operating system. Unfortunately for the accountants (often operating in their guise of management consultants), libraries do not exist simply to perform efficiently. The performance metaphor begins to break down when we look at what the service is trying to achieve and how well it is doing (or moving beyond easily measured 'outputs'). In suggesting a way forward, we would like to stress that performance measurement based on system efficiency is important for libraries and should run alongside any work on evaluating impact. Efficiency is important – but so is effectiveness.

Figure 2.1 (overleaf) outlines the traditional performance evaluation model. In this model, performance indicators are arrived at by looking successively at inputs, processes and outputs. Pursuing the engineering example, if you are in the business of manufacturing televisions, your inputs can be all the components that go together to make televisions. The processes will then be everything that you do in your production line to assemble the televisions. Your outputs are the completed and working televisions. In this model, if you want to look at the outcomes from the production process you can resort to aggregated outputs, by counting the total number of television sets produced (and probably also the proportion of these that work when switched on!).

The engineering process model works reasonably well in complex organizations like libraries – but only up to a point. No amount of aggregation in library settings will usually tell you much about impact. Our next example shows where the problem lies.

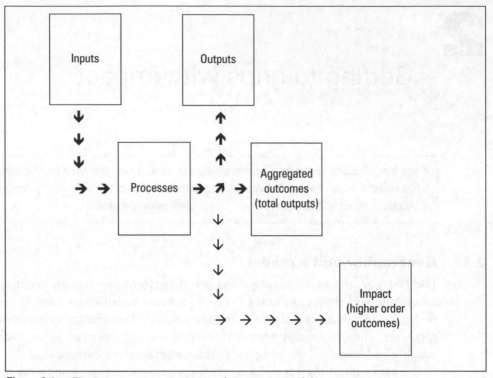

Figure 2.1   *The input, process, output and outcomes model*

If, for example, you are trying to improve the knowledge of a targeted group of children, you might do this by identifying and buying a collection of books on relevant topics and noting how many items you have bought at what cost (*input measures*). You will then prepare the books for loan and do whatever else is needed to get them into places where they are likely to be accessible to the target children (you might look at the speed and precision with which you do this as *process measures*).

Most of these books will then be used by some or all of the target group and you can choose various ways of measuring how frequently they are borrowed by these children (*output measures*). But how do you get from there to finding out whether the children know more as a result of your intervention? No amount of monitoring of book loans, however carefully done, will tell you whether the items borrowed were actually read, let alone whether the targeted users were in any way affected by what they read, or whether they learnt anything. In other words, in organizations dedicated to providing services for people, *aggregated outputs* are not usually the same as *outcomes*.

Some people in the performance indicators business have recognized this problem and tend to resort to other descriptions, such as *higher order outcomes* (or *achievement* in the education world) to describe the world of impact beyond traditional performance measurement. However, recognizing and labelling the problem area doesn't take us very much further. Approaching impact from this direction makes it difficult to focus clearly because most of the evidence gathered is only tangentially relevant, since it concentrates on the efficiency of systems, services and processes. That is why we take a different approach to evaluating impact in this book.

LAWS OF IMPACT EVALUATION 1
Effective impact evaluation requires clear and consistent use of terms.

2.2   Why is impact such a slippery concept?

It is not surprising if library service managers find it difficult to get to grips with issues about service impact. Full-time academic researchers often run into difficulty with these issues too. We recently did an evaluation (Streatfield and Markless, 2002a) of a whole national research programme, which was devoted to gauging the value and impact of various types of libraries, and found:

- little attempt to define terms
- no frameworks through which to explore value and impact
- a tendency to move away from value and impact towards reporting and describing activities/processes
- a linked tendency to escape from these problems into national surveys of activities or policies – which tell us almost nothing about value or impact
- problems with the methods chosen to gather evidence about impact.

Why has the library and information research community made little progress in this area? Part of the problem may be in yawning gaps between the demands of policy makers, the needs of service managers and the interests of academic researchers.
Broadly:

- Policy makers are being called upon to find better ways of assessing the benefits of their initiatives and programmes, and the quest to find mechanisms with which to control situations is still being pursued (this was first discussed as a research policy issue in the 1970s – see Caplan, Morrison and Stambaugh, 1975).
- Some parts of the public sector are more outcomes-focused (e.g. education, where there is heavy emphasis on comparative educational attainment); some areas are *aspiring* to become more outcomes driven (e.g. health and social care).
- The 'natural' interests of the library and information research community are in exploring and understanding social processes in depth. These may have to give way to the outcomes focus demanded by the 'new managerialism', but this battle has hardly begun.

What is clear is that policy makers, managers, practitioners and researchers will all come under increasing pressure to get to grips with questions of service value and impact. This will require a significant change in how research is conducted. *All* the projects that we looked at in our overview baulked at addressing educational-outcomes impact issues (such as 'before and after' measurements of skills acquisition). Researchers in other practice areas such as education, health and social care manage to conduct such studies. It can be done!

2.3   Overviews of impact

This book is focused on evaluating the impact (or, if you like, 'micro-impact') of your library but there is, of course, a bigger picture, which we will call 'macro-impact'. It is possible to concentrate on the overall economic or social impact of library and information systems for advocacy purposes. Three examples of this approach are the *Public Library Benefits Valuation Study* conducted by Glen Holt of the St Louis Public Library and colleagues (Holt et al., 2001), which concentrates on the perceived economic value of services to representatives of the communities served; *The Impact of School Library Media Centres on Achievement* by Lance, Welborn and Hamilton-Pennell (1993) and Lance and Loertscher (2002), in which links between good school libraries and student exam performance were established; and the Ohio study led by Ross Todd and Carol Kuhlthau (2005), which set out to answer the question 'How do school libraries/media resource centers help students with their learning in and away from school?' – by asking them directly. The Rutgers University team in effect orchestrated a mass write-in among high school students in Ohio to an electronic questionnaire, enlisting the help of targeted schools and school librarians. More than 13,000 students responded, many of them giving powerful testimony to the value of school libraries, as reported by Whelan (2004).

When you are assembling evidence of the impact of services it is important to remember that well grounded research evidence can and should be cited to back up your case – it isn't always necessary to reinvent the wheel. You can also use what we know from the research evidence to decide what areas to concentrate on in evaluation work, as we will show in the next chapter.

2.4   Changing how we think of evidence

2.4.1   From hypothesis testing to 'grounded theory'

What we now think of as scientific research is heavily shaped by Karl Popper's proposition that knowledge accumulates by falsification (or refutation) of hypotheses. In the social sciences, the idea of proposing hypotheses has been more or less readily accepted. Unfortunately, the complexities of doing research in the real world, where it is not possible to isolate and examine variables in turn, has led to perversion of Popper's approach in two ways. First, researchers drift into hypothesis-proving rather than hypothesis-challenging; this results in assembling evidence in favour of the hypothesis rather than making rigorous efforts to undermine it. Second, there is a tendency in social science research to rewrite or tinker with the hypotheses during the course of the research, when the work begins to call them into question. Both of these approaches fall foul of Popper's (1969) admonition that 'indefatigable rational criticism of our suppositions . . . is of decisive importance . . . to save us from the allure of the "obvious truth" of received doctrine'.

One answer to the perceived limitations of the hypothesis-based approach to social science research was proposed by Glaser and Strauss as long ago as 1967. Their concept of 'grounded theory' suggests that the theory should come out of qualitative-research data collection rather than being proposed at the outset. Researchers have welcomed 'grounded theory' because it gets them out of the hypothesis strait-jacket. Unfortunately, some researchers (including academic researchers in the library and information field) think of it as a licence to by-pass the difficult research questions and to claim that their evidence supports whatever ideas they want to advance. In fact, grounded theory offers a systematic approach based on constant comparisons, theoretical sampling and application of coding procedures.

Since much of the evidence-gathering likely to be undertaken by library-service managers is based on deciding in advance what to collect and how the results will be analysed, thinking about grounded theory raises a variety of questions about the nature of evidence and its interpretation. Not surprisingly, we will return to these questions in Chapter 8.

2.4.2 Illuminative evaluation

Malcolm Parlett and various collaborators have applied the kind of thinking that led to 'grounded theory' when looking at the particular issues of educational evaluation. Their solution, 'illuminative evaluation', is a flexible methodology that capitalizes on available resources and opportunities and draws upon different techniques to fit the total circumstances of each study (Parlett and Dearden, 1977).

They challenge the idea that evaluation should necessarily be centred upon student test scores and other performance data and that statements of objectives are an essential precondition for evaluation. The aims of illuminative evaluation are:

> to study the innovative programme: how it operates; how it is influenced by the various [educational] situations in which it is applied; what those directly concerned regard as its advantages and disadvantages; and how students' intellectual tasks and academic experiences are most affected. It attempts to discover and document what it is like to be participating in the scheme, whether as teacher or pupil; and . . . to discern and discuss the innovation's most significant features, recurring concomitants and critical processes. In short, it seeks to address and to illuminate a complex array of questions.   (Parlett and Hamilton, 1972)

What does this approach entail? There are usually three stages: investigator observation, further inquiry and then seeking to explain. As the same authors explain:

During the first, exploratory stage, we . . . become 'knowledgeable' about the scheme. At the second stage this [enables] our questioning to become more focused; communication to be more coherent and relaxed; and, in general, observation and enquiry to be more directed, systematic, and selective.

Elsewhere, they describe this phase as one of 'progressive focusing':

The third stage [involves] seeking general principles underlying the organization of the programme, spotting patterns of cause and effect within its operation, and placing individual findings within a broader explanatory context.

They admit that the extensive use of open-ended techniques for exploring the programme, progressive focusing and using qualitative data in illuminative evaluation

still raises the possibility of gross partiality on the part of the investigator. A number of precautionary tactics are possible. During the investigation different techniques can be used to cross-check the most important findings; open-ended material can be coded and checked by outside researchers; consultants to the evaluation can be charged with challenging preliminary interpretations. . . .

This approach is put forward in deliberate challenge to the 'traditional evaluator' who:

examines the . . . formalised plan and extracts the programme's goals, objectives or desired outcomes. From these, in turn, he derives the tests and attitude inventories he will administer. His aim is to evaluate the instructional system by examining whether, for example, it has 'attained its objectives' or met its 'performance criteria'.   (Parlett and Hamilton, 1972)

What attitude do we take to illuminative evaluation in this book? Although we have some difficulty with the claim that this and similar approaches in other disciplines constitute a new research paradigm (Reason and Rowan, 1981), we are certainly in sympathy with the general approach and have based our national school libraries research on this methodology (see Chapter 3). We also share Parlett and Hamilton's view that no research methods are immune from prejudice, experimenter bias and human error. Further, we recognize that no evidence-collection approach gives actual evidence of impact – the best we can hope for are strong surrogates for impact (that is, strong indicators that impact is occurring).

   The approach to impact evaluation outlined in this book starts from the position of the 'traditional evaluator', because setting objectives for programmes of service provision is an integral part of much service planning. Like Parlett and Hamilton, however, we favour cross-checking in data collection methods ('triangulation' in social science research jargon) because all evidence-collection methods have inherent weaknesses which may distort the results. We strongly favour employing a range of types of evidence, from the statistical to the anecdotal, in addressing impact and recognize that no amount of evaluation will ever provide the full and complete picture or explanation of a programme of service provision and its effects. In terms of reporting the evidence and conclusions, we again like the illuminative evaluators' concept of 'recognition of authority' as more helpful than 'objectivity' and 'generalizability' in weighing up evidence. (We use the word 'resonance' for the recognition by practitioners of what is being described in a setting in which they work.) All these points are explored in later chapters.

2.5 What does impact mean?

What form does impact evaluation take in the real world of libraries? Here are some real examples drawn from different sectors of library and information work in the UK. Not all of these cover 'conventional' evidence of library service impact.

Example 2.1 The health service

It can be difficult for UK health libraries to demonstrate their impact on patient care as required by the Government. Usually, they can only point to general benefits of their work on the people who are, in turn, influencing delivery or providing services directly to patients. However, sometimes they are lucky. When the health librarian at one hospital tries to find out about the usefulness of the interlibrary loans service to clinical staff he arranges a series of interviews with users. One of these users, a psychologist, reports that he has cut the waiting time before his patients can see him from two years to six months, as a direct consequence of the information provided. This type of evidence fits well into the health culture, since there are specific 'quality of patient care' government targets about cutting waiting lists. The only problem is how best to present this story to senior managers who may be more accustomed to assessing quantitative performance data (Chamberlain, 2003).

Example 2.2 The world of business

One of the major UK employers' organizations operates a proactive library and information service for its staff. At the period in question, one target user group for this service is the staff of the regional offices scattered around the country. These people operate more or less independently but they are brought in to the London headquarters once a year for a week of briefing and de-briefing. Since they are an eccentric bunch of individuals, it is no surprise that this week always culminates in a party of legendary proportions. This event usually takes in half a dozen drinking places, but also sucks in a few key members of HQ staff – strictly by invitation only. The head of the information service is first invited to join this gathering in his second year of running the service. This is a strong endorsement of the perceived value of the service by this maverick group and, accordingly, useful evidence to the manager that he is on the right lines. Unfortunately, this evidence is not likely to feature in any official report, especially since his line manager doesn't get invited!

Example 2.3   Schools

A school librarian wants to find out what the children think of the school's homework club (designed to support them when they are doing assignments or preparing for lessons outside school hours). She wants to know why some children drop out and why others never attend. After piloting a questionnaire, she chooses three groups (regulars, drop outs, non-attendees) in one year cohort for a survey. The survey shows that the most effective promotion for the club has come from teachers and fellow students (rather than from posters or leaflets); the student monitors (older students) are strongly disliked; access to staff help is valued over access to resources; and a picture emerges of how the homework club contributes to effective curriculum delivery.

As a result of these findings the monitors have been rapidly eased out. Tutors are now equipped with homework club bookmarks for use on academic review days and parents' evenings, so that the club can be offered as a place of help and so that attendance can be set as a target when action is discussed. Extra teacher support time is given to the club and specific support is planned to help the more vulnerable students when they attend. The result has been a steady core of attendance that no longer changes dramatically from season to season.

This is a classic approach to evaluation – it is time consuming because it is thorough and it has provided the whole school (not just the librarian) with evidence on which to make decisions. The effect has also been to reinforce the role of the librarian in supporting curriculum development (Streatfield and Markless, 2003).

Example 2.4   Higher education

Infoquest is a learning resource linked to specific courses, using a virtual learning environments approach to enable large cohorts of students to enhance their information-handling skills (Helm, 2003). It is being developed by Sheffield Hallam University in England as part of a larger e-learning initiative.

Since this work is financed through teaching and learning enhancement funds, the concern is to demonstrate that it is having real impact on student learning. If the programme succeeds it should make the information-literacy work of librarians more tangible for academics and create opportunities for collaboration and integration (Webber, 2003). Consequently, the evaluation of this programme concentrates on the benefits to students and academic staff. The evaluation work done so far includes interviews with students conducted while they are using the resource, and interviews with academic staff, focusing on student work; a small number of students also keep learning diaries.

The outcomes reported by academic staff include better quality student assignments, improvements in referencing, in the range of resources cited and in the quality of student argument. Students report that Infoquest offers a safe learning environment; they find it flexible (they can use it when the need arises); and claim that they are learning by using Infoquest and are developing their skills. This type of evidence is crucial when we are expected to demonstrate that needs are being met in order to account for funds received (and to prepare the way for further funding bids). More specifically, the evidence so far shows that Infoquest is becoming integrated into student learning and that the system is able to deal with the large number of students involved.

3

The research base of this work

> If your main aim now is to get to grips with impact evaluation in your library, you may like to skip this chapter. On the other hand, if you are interested in what the literature has to say about impact evaluation and, more specifically, if you want to know about the research that underpins this book – please read on.

This chapter looks at some of the main recent advances in evaluating impact in other sectors, how these have influenced our thinking and how they can help library-service managers in evaluating impact. We then home in on the library and information research and what it tells us about the overall impact of various types of libraries. Finally, we outline the research base of our own work leading to this book.

3.1   What we know about impact from the management literature

Fortunately, perhaps, we don't have space here to trace all the twists and turns of researchers and management gurus who moved on from traditional performance measurement in a quest to determine the impact of services. Instead, we will look at a few important staging posts along the way.

We have pointed to a shift in focus, away from monitoring processes and outputs using traditional performance indicators (busy-ness statistics) towards 'higher-order outcomes', 'impact' or 'achievement' – or from monitoring efficiency to assessing effectiveness. Earlier we noted the danger of adopting too narrow a focus on value for money or costs as *the* determining factor. The two approaches described below arose out of concern to get a broad perspective on effectiveness and to translate this into practical evaluation action. Both versions were generated in the world of business and both are sufficiently widely used to make it worth considering them here.

3.1.1   The balanced scorecard

A useful way of ensuring *balance* in generating indicators comes in the form of the 'balanced scorecard'. This approach was developed in business in the USA as a result of concern that:

because traditional measurement systems have sprung from the finance function, the systems have a control bias. That is, traditional performance measurement systems specify the particular actions they want employees to take and then measure to see whether the employees have in fact taken those actions. In that way, the systems try to control behavior. Such measurement systems fit with the engineering mentality of the Industrial Age.

The balanced scorecard, on the other hand . . . puts strategy and vision, not control, at the center. It establishes goals but assumes that people will adopt whatever behaviors and take whatever actions are necessary to arrive at those goals. (Kaplan and Norton, 1992)

Although developed in the business sector, this system provides a useful framework to consult when you are trying to draw up performance measures for the library. The underlying premise is that no single measure (whether financial in business or levels of use in libraries) can focus attention on all critical areas of the service. However, it can be difficult to design a balanced set of measures that gives a comprehensive overview on your own. The balanced scorecard sets out to provide help in this area. It:

allows managers to look at the business from four important perspectives [and yet] minimizes information overload by limiting the number of measures used. . . . The balanced scorecard forces managers to focus on the handful of measures that are most critical.

The scorecard approach is based on answering four fundamental questions:

- How do customers (users) see us?
- What must we excel at? (internal perspective)
- Can we continue to improve and create value? (innovation and learning perspective)
- How do we look to shareholders? (or stakeholders – financial perspective).

Answering these questions *together* lets you see 'whether improvements in one area may have been achieved at the expense of another'. Even the best objectives can be achieved badly. Using this approach means that you can consider together disparate elements of the competitive agenda such as becoming more customer-orientated, shortening response times, improving stock quality, emphasizing teamwork and developing new services. Viewing performance and management become more rounded. You do not just pursue loans, customer satisfaction or expenditure on fiction in isolation.

The idea behind the scorecard is to formulate targets in each of the four areas below (3–5 targets in each) and to design one or more measures for each 'goal'.

Customer perspective (users)
Customer concerns tend to fall into four categories: time, quality, performance and service, and cost.

You need to articulate goals for each of these four areas and then translate the goals into specific measures.

Internal perspective

Managers need to focus on these critical internal operations that enable them to meet and satisfy customer needs.

This part of the scorecard looks at the processes and competencies at which you must excel, for example technological capability; introduction of new ideas; skills, monitoring/evaluation/consultation mechanisms.

Innovation and learning perspective

This looks at the organization's ability to grow, learn, develop and introduce new services. It focuses on measures such as take-up of new services; and time taken to develop and introduce new approaches.

Financial perspective

One company 'stated its financial goals [as] simply "to survive", to succeed, to prosper'. For some library services, such as Schools Library Services in the UK, measures like cash flow, growth in customer base, and income by services provided or by school, are critical.

[Selected quotes are from Kaplan and Norton, 1992 and 1993.]

3.1.2   Business Excellence Model

The Business Excellence Model promoted by the European Foundation for Quality Management offers a structured approach to organizational self-assessment. Although the model started life in the private sector, it has been adapted for public-sector working, and is being adopted in local government. In 1999 we conducted a UK survey in which 16 public library services reported that their authority was using a version of this model. There is growing evidence of government interest in this model within Europe as a means of enacting a 'continuous service improvement' agenda, especially in relation to outcome-based benchmarking.

The main premise of this model, expressed in its nine criteria and 32 sub-criteria, is that:

> Customer satisfaction, people (staff) satisfaction and a positive impact on society, are achieved through leadership driving force and strategy, people management, resources and processes, leading, ultimately, to excellence in results.   (Brigham, 1999)

This model was one of the starting points for a self-assessment process specifically designed for library-service managers and staff developers as part of the research project led by Margaret Kinnell and Bob Usherwood, two of the leading academics in the UK field (Usherwood, Evans and Jones, 1999). The resulting book (Kinnell, Usherwood and Jones, 1999a) is accompanied by a separately published training pack and tool kit (Kinnell, Usherwood and Jones, 1999b) containing 'all the necessary documents for developing a training programme and undertaking a self-assessment within a public information and library service'.

Their version of the model, which also incorporated elements of two other frameworks, offers ten criteria (or managerial domains):

Leadership	Processes
Policy and strategy	Customer satisfaction
Customer focus	Employee satisfaction
Employee management	Impact on society
Resource management	Overall performance

These elements are then sub-divided and a set of issues for exploration is linked to each. Although potentially useful for systematic planning purposes this is an inherently complex model: who is likely to keep all the criteria, let alone sub-criteria, and issues in their heads? Accordingly, we have opted for a more straightforward approach to evaluating the impact of services for managerial and accountability purposes. However, as organizations get more involved in evaluating impact they may well find both the balanced scorecard and the business excellence model useful to ensure that they are working systematically and not avoiding key criteria.

3.1.3 More models

When academics engage with impact evaluation it is quite common for them to try to turn the results into models or research instruments for other people to use. There is only space here to mention two of these ventures.

SERVQUAL

Evaluating service quality in the retail sector has spawned a literature of its own. One of the best-known instruments (despite its horrible acronym) is *SERVQUAL*, which aims to measure perceptions of any service across the five service-quality dimensions identified by Parasuraman, Zeithaml and Berry (1988) as: tangibles, reliability, responsiveness, assurance and empathy. Some of the fundamental difficulties in trying to apply an instrument using this approach have been identified by Robinson and Pidd (1998), who find that:

The only areas of agreement appear to be that service quality is an attitude and is distinct from customer satisfaction, that perceptions of performance need to be measured, that the number and definition of dimensions depends on the service context, and that negatively worded statements should be avoided.

They conclude that: 'Following a decade of measurement with SERVQUAL is it possible that another decade will follow? The answer is probably not.'

Why does SERVQUAL rate a mention if it is now being found wanting? There is a strong tendency by national governments and others to try to produce 'simple' sets of impact indicators that can be universally applied. A generation of SERVQUAL evaluation demonstrates that such a 'one size fits all' approach is hugely problematic.

Inspiring Learning for All

The Inspiring Learning for All framework, sponsored by and developed for the (UK) Museums, Libraries and Archives Council, claims to set out 'what an accessible and inclusive museum, archive or library that stimulates and supports learning looks like'. This framework is primarily intended to cover informal learning and includes an impact evaluation dimension driven by a set of generic learning outcomes, apparently derived from the educational evaluation literature, which are described as 'a new research tool to measure learning'. These generic learning outcomes (or impact areas) focus on 'Knowledge and understanding', 'Skills', 'attitudes and values', 'Enjoyment, inspiration, creativity' (all of which are areas where we can expect to have an impact, as we will show later) and 'Activity, behaviour and progression'. The framework is extensive, and offers help in developing research tools (including a tool bank), in coding and analysing data, and in presenting evidence. (See www.inspiringlearningforall.gov.uk/.)

3.1.4   Educational views on impact

One important source of ideas on evaluating services, which we drew upon heavily in our early work on impact, is the literature on monitoring effectiveness and quality in education. This literature predates the current obsession with managing performance and focuses on some key elements that have become central to our model for evaluating impact, notably Fitz-Gibbon's (1996) views on the vital importance of:

- starting with some view of the characteristics and achievements of an effective service (what does a quality library service look like?)
- high quality information (both qualitative and quantitative) about the services and systems that is specific to your local context – to enable rational decisions to be taken about change and external pressures
- good quality performance indicators (to enable constant checking of service performance)

- designing these indicators because they are rarely readily available
- revisiting performance indicators as more information is gathered, to check that they are still credible and doing the intended job.

The work in education continues to inform our thinking. Recent ideas in education about evidence-informed practice and, even more importantly, practice-based evidence (Eraut, 2004), as well as about the role of the practitioner researcher in generating valid data, are central to self-evaluation using the model that we present in this book.

3.2 Evidence-based practice and the LIS picture

Are library services having any impact overall and, if so, how are people finding out about it? Why does this matter? We need to know what it is possible to achieve and how, so that we can concentrate our efforts where they can be seen to have an effect. It's also important to know how this impact is being evaluated, so that we don't waste time trying to collect information in areas where it is too difficult to make progress or where we can't get at the evidence.

Looking at the evidence should help us to broaden our ideas about what can be made to work and how we can evaluate it. Library managers may be reluctant to engage with service impact if they are unsure what this encompasses and if it looks as though the evidence will be hard to get. Some of these concerns may be reduced by seeing that other people have 'been there and done that'. We hope that the next section will add to your ideas about what you can look at and how.

We referred in Chapter 1 to the beginnings of evidence-based working in the library and information service field. One way in which this manifests itself is through reviews[1] of the research literature. Until fairly recently there was little attempt in the library world to conduct systematic or semi-systematic reviews[1] of the research literature, so that it was difficult to say what the research was telling us overall. Recent semi-systematic reviews of school libraries (Williams, Wavell and Coles 2001; Williams, Coles and Wavell, 2002; Lonsdale 2003) and of the research on the impact of museums, archives and libraries (Wavell et al., 2002), as well as a systematic review of health libraries (Weightman and Williamson, 2005), have improved this picture and other reviews are being commissioned.

So what do we know about the impact of various types of libraries and information services? How much does the research literature tell us about the impact of libraries, as distinct from efficiency on the one hand or, on the other, advocacy reports that start from the premise that libraries are a good thing? The short version is:

- a good deal if you are interested in *school libraries*
- quite a lot about *health libraries*
- rather less but in a growing volume for *further and higher education libraries*
- a patchy picture for *public libraries* – some interesting overview (macro-impact) work, a series of research projects beginning to point the way towards finding out about

the social impact of public libraries and a growing body of evidence about the usefulness of reading promotion projects
• rather less if you are interested in *workplace libraries* or in *mediated information service* provision (where the information specialist, frequently a specialist in the relevant subject area, works with the enquirer to address the problem).

Although strictly beyond the confines of this book, there is also interesting research being conducted on:

• *user needs* of particular groups of information users. Much of this was conducted in earlier decades, including experimental design and development of specialist information services for social workers, education administrators, sexual health workers and others, using variations on the action research approach
• modelling or interpreting the *information-seeking behaviour of users*, shortly to be brought together in a single publication aimed (unsurprisingly) at researchers (Fisher, Erdelez and McKechnie, forthcoming).

The main research findings about the impact of libraries is summarized in a little more detail below.

3.3   The overall research picture

In this brief overview we draw heavily on the literature reviews cited in the previous section, teasing out libraries from museums and archives where necessary. The study by Wavell et al. (2002) was funded by the UK's Museums, Libraries and Archives Council (in its previous guise as Resource) and consisted largely of a review of the literature published during a five year retrospective period, with a particular emphasis on impact evaluations conducted within the UK. It did, however, include major research in the USA and Australia.

Looking across all this work, they conclude that libraries have 'an impact on *personal development*. There is also a current emphasis on the impact evaluation of *special projects and initiatives*'.

This judgement leads them to the conclusion that: 'a shift in emphasis towards the evaluation of core services will require a corresponding shift in professional thinking'.

3.3.1   Overall impact: economic vitality

Commenting on the broad issue of the economic effects of library services, Wavell and her colleagues judge that 'the research is at the stage of investigating possible approaches to measuring impact and demonstrating potential rather than actual impact'. They find that:

• studies examining *special libraries* have shown that they provide information that can have a positive impact on professional decision-making

- research into economic impact in *public libraries* cited evidence of impact in terms of:

  — direct and indirect impact on jobs
  — respondents' willingness to pay for services
  — respondents' perceptions of economic benefits to the local community.

In their view:

> The research is at the stage of investigating possible approaches to measuring impact and demonstrating potential rather than actual impact. . . . the economic impact of information to the business community cannot be quantified at present and . . . the contribution of company . . . libraries in providing that information is not readily quantifiable.

They also make a series of significant points about doing economic impact research involving libraries:

- studies examining *economic* impact sometimes use relatively complex analytical techniques and are conducted by economists or special consultants
- some studies use qualitative and quantitative approaches in which economic impact is not necessarily defined in monetary terms
- economic impact of the sector is dependent upon data sources that are often incomplete, inaccurate or unavailable
- research concentrates on the public sector and major public spending initiatives
- research into the economic impact and value of *business information* is limited
- research into the relationship between *public libraries* and town centre regeneration is limited.

They observe that 'much of the evidence is in fact pointing to potential areas of impact rather than actual impact'.

The British Library recently published the results of an economic impact study which seeks to quantify both the direct and indirect benefits of their services to the nation (Spectrum, 2004). They use the 'contingent valuation' approach to cost-benefit analysis (previously applied in the St Louis Public Library study mentioned in Chapter 2) for part of this work. In this approach, respondents are asked either how much they are willing to pay for services, or to what extent they are willing to accept compensation for not having the services (usually expressed in terms of amounts of reduction in taxes). Inevitably, both modes of questioning tend to encourage polarization of opinions, and they have other limitations, which are explored by Holt et al. (1996).

3.3.2   Overall impact: libraries and learning

Wavell and colleagues identify several empirical studies examining the relationship between libraries and learning, focused on reader development in public libraries or school libraries, or on support for learning through reading development in young children and after-school activities.

They aver that evidence from research into learning and library use indicates a positive impact on:

- enjoyment and choice of leisure reading material
- reading development in young children
- academic achievement, particularly in terms of language skills
- acquisition of skills, particularly ICT and information literacy
- broader aspects of learning, such as increased motivation for learning, self confidence and independence.

Their review 'identified greater potential for impact than was actually substantiated by the evidence, particularly in terms of knowledge and understanding'.

They judge that:

> Academic libraries in the FE and HE [further and higher education] sectors are also concerned with tackling the issue of impact assessment and, at present, are at the stage of attempting to find appropriate indicators and data collection techniques.

3.3.3   Public libraries

Social impact

Evidence from seven UK projects cited by Wavell and colleagues indicates positive impact of public libraries in supporting:

- personal development – including formal education, lifelong learning and training; after-school activities; literacy, leisure, social and cultural objectives through book borrowing; and skills development and availability of public information. (Studies concentrating on specific aspects of service provision, such as ICT, indicate that these services also contribute.)
- social cohesion – by providing a meeting place and centre of community development; raising the profile and confidence of marginalized groups
- community empowerment – by supporting community groups and developing a sense of equity and access
- local culture and identity – by providing community identity and information
- health and well-being – by contributing to the quality of life and how well people feel, as well as providing health information services
- local economy – by providing business information and supporting skills development.

They decide that the most compelling evidence is 'in the area of personal development, if only because the immediate outcomes are more easily identified and less problematic in terms of establishing causality'.

However, they also decide that, taken together, the exploratory research projects 'suggest the mechanisms for monitoring social impact in public libraries have yet to be established'.

3.3.4 Health libraries

Building on an earlier review by Patrick O'Connor (2002), Weightman and Williamson (2005) conclude that

> *health care libraries* can influence patient outcomes in various ways:
>
> * rapid diagnosis
> * appropriate investigation(s) and choice of drug(s)
> * reduced length of stay in hospitals
> * avoiding hospital-acquired infection
> * avoiding additional outpatient visits
>
> [and that] . . . clinical librarian and other library services can also result in savings of health professionals' time.

They note that

> much of this recent research has been based on case-studies, including critical event analyses, and cross-sectional surveys. These are the most practical study methods but the available research is of variable quality and does not always minimise the potential for bias.

Wavell and her colleagues similarly conclude that good quality information provision has a positive effect on clinical decision-making.

3.3.5 School libraries

Those studies found by Wavell and colleagues that examine the association between library provision and academic achievement in schools (including several important US studies) identify factors that appear to enhance the impact on young people's learning. These include:

* readily available, high quality resources
* an appropriate environment
* the presence of trained library staff.

The research also highlights the need for effective partnerships between library professionals, teachers, health workers and parents in order to mediate and facilitate the learning process.

For people who want to know more about the impact of school libraries, we recommend the research paper *School Libraries Work!* (Scholastic, 2004). This is an interesting mix of advocacy assertions and (good) summaries of the current research evidence.[2]

Since there is probably more evidence available about school libraries worldwide than about any other type of library it is probably worth adding some detail, based largely on our own review of the research (Streatfield and Markless, 2002b):

* *It is clear that school libraries can make a real contribution to teaching and learning.* Libraries/librarians can help build independence in learning, foster study and information-handling (problem solving) skills, help motivate pupils to learn, offer conditions that encourage absorption in the task and promote self-esteem. There is now a strong body of evidence from academic research and from project evaluations to show what *processes* work and how in these areas.
* We do not yet have direct systematic evidence to show how school libraries *add value through these processes* although school managers and teachers consistently report that they do.
* As already noted, a cluster of controlled studies on attainment outcomes has been conducted in the USA. These studies show that *school libraries do make a positive difference to attainment* and indicate how. They also show that it is possible to measure these differences. However, there are problems in transferring these findings to other national settings because the approaches to providing school libraries differ. There are, for example, variations in the range of services usually offered by US media resource centres and UK school libraries, as well as in the required professional education, in the usual terms of employment and in school expectations of librarians.

In what areas do school libraries make a difference? Earlier UK research on effectiveness in school library provision identified eight areas in which the school library could have a positive effect on teaching and learning:

* the learning environment/ethos
* variety of learning experience
* supporting systematic skills development and research
* access to a wider world of information
* encouraging and supporting learning
* differentiation/equal access to the curriculum
* self esteem and the independent learner
* careers guidance.   (based on Streatfield and Markless, 1994)

More recent Scottish research (Williams and Wavell, 2001) has amplified many of these messages. Their work focused on:

- **motivation for learning**, such as expression of enthusiasm, absorption in the task
- **progression in learning**, specific skills relating to information handling, ICT, reading, study skills and new knowledge – such as the ability to make notes, cite references, etc.
- **independence in learning**, following on from progression after a task or skill is mastered – confidence and competence to continue unaided, applying skills learnt elsewhere in the curriculum, confidence to seek help and increased self esteem
- **interaction in learning**, such as peer co-operation, discussion about a task, use of appropriate behaviour.

Back in the USA, *Project Achievement* (see Loertscher with Todd, 2003) reviews the research to identify the areas in which the school library can make a difference, in order to guide school librarians towards more effective working. They specify:

- developing skilled and avid readers
- making learners information-literate
- building high quality learning experiences for learners through collaboration with teachers
- building an information-rich environment and enhancing teaching and learning through ICT.

These and related themes are being picked up in current research in the USA and Australia.

3.3.6 Workplace libraries

Wavell and colleagues find evidence that provision of information by special libraries can have a positive impact on professional decision-making.

3.4 What we don't know

The problem at this fairly early stage of moving towards evidence-based library and information work is that there are still aspects that have not been properly investigated – where what we are doing is what feels right or what we have always done rather than what we know works or can be made to work. These gaps in the research may occur because nobody is challenging us to show our worth, because the right questions haven't been asked yet or because the results so far are inconclusive.

Looking at library research on impact generally, we can currently see:

- lots of descriptive and anecdotal evidence and descriptions of best practice
- little detail of data-gathering methods; absence of systematic and rigorous reporting (this is a real issue for the field), and as a result
- often no way of identifying the quality of the data collection through the published reports

- lots of attention to *potential outcomes* rather than systematically assessed impact evidence
- some synopses of impact investigations, but not integrated into a growing body of evidence.

There are still some challenging impact questions waiting to be answered. For example:

- How big is the overall economic, social and educational contribution of libraries to the community?
- What mix of library services works best in different situations?
- What is the overall value of libraries to the country or to society?
- Is this value consistent over time?

These questions may appear to be too big to be addressed, but we already have some answers emerging to the first two of these in relation to school libraries and the third is being sporadically addressed, although so far without clear success.

Example 3.1 Playing for Success

This project demonstrates that we can learn useful lessons from other research areas. The Out of Hours Study Support Project is a UK national initiative, focused on providing homework facilities for schoolchildren, including some projects based in school libraries. National evaluation shows positive impact on academic attainment by the students involved, as well as improved attitudes to school and better attendance at school (MacBeath et al., 2001).

The most rigorous evaluation, of Playing for Success work involving football clubs, encompasses observation, interviews with people involved, questionnaires to pupils, parents and schools, attitude measurement of pupils before and after involvement and tests of their reading and mental arithmetic (potentially a model for future library impact research?). The programme was popular with pupils, contributing to improved attitudes, motivation and self-esteem, and improved academic skills and achievement. School libraries offer a potential base for this type of support, and could aspire to achieve some of these results, even if they do not have the magnetic appeal of football clubs!

And finally

> National research evidence of impact does not have much effect at a local level. Heads, Governors etc. want to hear of local successes and local improvement. They want to see how their students are benefiting. . . . You will not be heard until your day-to-day practice is evidence-based; a practice that is directed towards demonstrating the real power of your contribution to the school's learning goals.
>
> (Todd, 2001)

3.5 Where our model comes from

All of this research provides a context for our own work, which concentrates on helping library managers to get to grips with service impact. What follows now is an attempt to trace our learning path through a series of national research and development projects over the past 20 years.

3.5.1 Getting at impact through research and development

As with many projects, the early stages in developing this model were largely accidental. In the 1980s the authors worked together on UK national research and development focused on what is now usually called information literacy. Since this work was conducted in schools and further education colleges it was no great surprise that we became very interested in how their libraries contributed to the central activities of their institutions. Our interest was soon translated into another national research project, The Effective School Library, in which we concentrated on the roles of the library staff in the key part of their job, supporting teaching and learning. Our choice of focus forced us to address the issues involved in evaluating the impact of these services in schools (Streatfield and Markless, 1994).

In the final stages of this project we devised sets of performance indicators to help librarians decide where to focus in order to make a positive contribution to teaching and learning in their schools. We quickly realized that it is vital to make direct links between activities and impact. Failure to make these links has led generations of school librarians to pursue a vision of what we now caricature as the 'All-singing, all-dancing learning resource centre designed to support students as independent learners' – or 'the Holy Grail model'. This approach is fine if the school as a whole is committed to a student-centred approach to learning, but our research clearly showed that this model of library provision won't work if the school puts a strong emphasis on traditional teaching. This project taught us valuable lessons about the need to base development decisions on a clear view of the impact you can achieve or want to achieve.

Next, we turned our attention to the role of the further education college library/resource centre, in another nation project imaginatively entitled The Effective College Library (Streatfield and Markless, 1997). As part of this project we decided to work with seven college libraries in which the staff had already decided to innovate in an aspect of support for teaching and learning (ranging from running information skills workshops to assigning library staff to work as part of curriculum teams). Since each innovation was different, there was a real chance of a mess, with all the libraries going off in different directions. What we needed was a process to help people to decide together what they mean by impact and how impact can be evaluated for their innovation. We designed a workshop for our collaborators and the process model was born! A common approach to generating performance indicators and targets duly emerged. Now we were in a position to start looking at the real impact of these services on students and teaching staff. Our chosen approach also meant that we were well placed to go further down the impact evaluation route by testing this methodology, trying out some performance indicators and evaluating the innovations within the same project (Markless and Streatfield, 2000).

By this time we were in full research flow. Our next opportunity to focus strongly on impact came with the National Year of Reading, a major programme to celebrate libraries and reading, promoted by the UK Government and mounted in 1998–99. We were asked to take on the evaluation of public library involvement in this programme, which saw public library services come back to the forefront of the public sector agenda after years of government-prompted neglect (Streatfield et al., 2000).

What was really striking when we attended various events organized in different parts of the country during the Year of Reading, was the level of energy flowing through the library staff and everyone else involved. It was obvious that the events were having a big impact – but when we asked what effect an event was having on the promotion of reading in the community we heard only vague answers. Yes, the Year of Reading seemed to be working, but nobody appeared to have much idea about how to evaluate its impact locally. Why was this?

We found the clue that led to the answer in the files of 147 annual public library service plans sent in to the relevant government department for England. Our team ploughed through all of these, looking for references to library managers' plans for the National Year of Reading and for the programme evaluation measures to be used to judge the results. There were plenty of plans for events during the Year of Reading, but most of these had no evaluation criteria attached and, where there were any, they were nearly always process performance indicators (numbers of activities, or targets for numbers of people to be involved). Almost everyone had backed away from the more difficult questions about evaluating impact.

Similarly, our national survey conducted as part of this evaluation found 26% of public library services in which managers reported that they had adopted some impact or achievement indicators or targets in relation to the Year of Reading. However, when we followed up by asking them to give examples, well over half proved to be process or output indicators.

3.5.2   Generating an impact evaluation model

We were now convinced that library service managers needed help to focus on impact, especially because they are coming under increasing pressure to do so. Not surprisingly, the Library and Information Commission took the same view! As a result, it funded us to do some development work concentrating on public libraries and on the schools library services that provide strategic help to individual schools in UK local authorities. For the Best Value and Better Performance in Libraries Project, we engaged the interest of various public library service and schools library services management teams with the offer to help them shape up their impact ideas. For this purpose we clearly needed a process and one that was robust enough to deal with a variety of services and settings. Fortunately, we had a model ready for this purpose.

We based the first of the workshops for library managers on the process that we originally devised for college librarians. Over the next few months, we tried out the processes on various management teams and collected feedback as we went along so that we could strengthen the model. At the end of the project we published the results as a set of guidance materials.[3]

Over the next four years we further refined the process model by running training workshops for a wide range of library service managers in all kinds of settings. We also ran or contributed to development projects based on the model for groups of health librarians developing specific innovations, children's librarians focusing on reader development and further education college librarians interested in benchmarking on the basis of service impact.

At the time of going to press we are near the end of year two of a rolling programme to help university library staff to evaluate the impact of their programmes and initiatives. The Impact Implementation Programme has so far helped ten university library teams to explore the impact of e-learning and e-implementation (Markless and Streatfield, 2005); now a further 12 universities are working through another annual cycle of workshops and practical impact evidence-gathering, looking at integrated enquiry services, e-information services, subject e-support for research, and support for a wider range of students.[4]

This approach to the generation of performance indicators and targets has helped a growing number of librarians and education managers to get to grips with the fairly complex issues and choices involved. It has also enabled librarians to engage in development planning from the right end – that is starting from specific time-limited objectives and moving on to set realistic and achievable targets.

3.5.3 Creating a self-evaluation process

Could a free-standing and comprehensive self-evaluation process be developed for libraries? It should be possible to do this, if we know enough about the optimum range of services possible, the key constraints and the main dimensions of process and impact evaluation for these services.

Fortunately, when we were asked (in 2003) to do this for school libraries by the UK Government's Department for Education and Skills, we felt that the research evidence about what works in schools was strong enough and that, with the help of 53 schools, we could come up with practical self-evaluation frameworks for primary (age 5 to 11) school libraries (Streatfield and Markless, 2004) and a more comprehensive and challenging version for secondary (11 to 18) schools (Markless and Streatfield, 2004).[5] The secondary model offers seven broad areas in which the school library can make a difference, breaks this down into segments, then takes the school library manager through a series of steps to arrive at an evaluation of that segment. Data collection tools are provided to help and the process is rounded off with guidance on how to do better in the chosen area. In some ways that ambitious project provided a dress-rehearsal for writing this book.

Notes

1   A distinction is drawn here between *systematic reviews* for weighing up
     published research evidence, which is a meticulous, exhaustive and expensive
     process, and *semi-systematic reviews*, which are less rigorous and usually only
     cover recent reports, but in which the selection criteria, scope and
     methodology are all specified. Systematic reviews, as developed by the
     Cochrane Collaboration in the health field and as applied to education, social
     care and other areas by the Campbell Collaboration and others, involve an
     apparatus of rigorous selection and operational processes, such as independent
     expert panels, double reviewing and systematic exclusion of reports that do
     not meet all the specifications.

2   One caveat is that the unnamed overview authors make an unfortunate claim
     about the important Ohio study, that '99.4% of students . . . believe school
     libraries and their services help them become better learners'. The percentage
     referred to the 13,000 plus students (an impressive number) who *chose* to
     contribute their views and send them in to the researchers – not something
     that people are likely to do to any extent if they have a bad experience of
     libraries.

3   The Best Value and Better Performance in Libraries Project was conducted by
     a consortium led by Information Management Associates and also involving
     David Haynes Associates, the London Borough of Hammersmith and Fulham
     and Wiltshire and Swindon Learning Resources. The project team consisted of
     David Streatfield, Sharon Markless and Ray Swan (IMA); Noeleen Cookman
     (DHA); David Herbert (Hammersmith); and Susan McCulloch (Wiltshire).
     The main output from this project can be found at the IMA website:
     www.informat.org (click on Best Value in the drop-down menu).

4   This programme is organised and led by the Library and Information Research
     Group and the Society of College, National and University Libraries.

5   These self-evaluation models and support materials were distributed widely to
     schools in England in the summer of 2004 and are available on the Teachernet
     website www.teachernet.gov.uk/schoollibraries. A version with specially written
     site navigation guidance can be found at www.informat.org (click on School
     Library Self-evaluation Model in the drop-down menu).

Part 2
Evaluating impact

4

Putting the impact into planning

This chapter introduces the model for evaluating impact and makes some points about how to use it. You are then invited to start using the model by thinking about the answers to some general questions. Answering these questions is an important step to take in moving into the impact evaluation model.

4.1 Why do we need a new evaluation model?

The balance between service delivery, detailed consideration of processes and impact evaluation is critical when assessing the success of a service. However, our experience suggests that the balance is usually heavily weighted away from impact evaluation. Ever since we first began to work systematically with library and information service managers on impact, two points have been apparent:

- **The concepts and terminology get in the way**. People easily become confused about such ideas as efficiency and effectiveness when they try to apply them in practice. Not only that but the terms used, such as inputs, processes, outputs and outcomes (and higher order outcomes) are applied inconsistently, both by managers in practice and in some of the published literature on performance evaluation.
- **When people identify an area for attention or improvement they can usually come up with a list of things to do to put it right**. Generally speaking however, people find it much harder to think about the aims and objectives underlying what they are trying to do (that is, what they are trying to achieve by providing services). Unfortunately, this focus on aims is necessary: we need to be very clear about what we are trying to achieve if we want to be able to tell whether we have succeeded. Since people are usually more comfortable with organizing and running activities, their focus on impact often gets fuzzy – when this happens we slide off into identifying process performance indicators (or 'tick off when done' indicators). These tell us whether things on the list have been done, but they don't tell us whether they were worth doing, or indeed whether they have had any effect.

Our response to these two challenges is to offer a process for people to work through to help to get to grips with impact. We have used this general approach with more than 700 library and information service managers and have adapted it for all kinds of settings – from school libraries to universities and from public libraries to business and industry.

The good news is that we know that this approach to evaluating impact works! People consistently tell us that our process helps them to work systematically through the issues without getting sidetracked or bogged down in the complexities. Now we are offering you a version of the same general process – please let us know how well it works for you by contacting us at www.facetpublishing.co.uk/evaluatingimpact. If you hit any problems that are not fully covered in this book, you may find that they have been dealt with on the website; if not, contact us there and we will try to help.

4.2   The model

We have adopted a step-by-step approach to generating impact indicators. The idea is that by working through the steps managers should emerge with a set of useful impact indicators linked to what they are trying to achieve. By the end of the process, you should also be well on the way to putting together a workable development plan and an implementation timetable to go with it, whether this is for a library service or for a research, development or pilot project. By the time you have worked through the model once, and have generated your own impact indicators, you will be able to integrate collecting evidence of impact into your planning cycle. The steps in the model are shown in Figure 4.1.

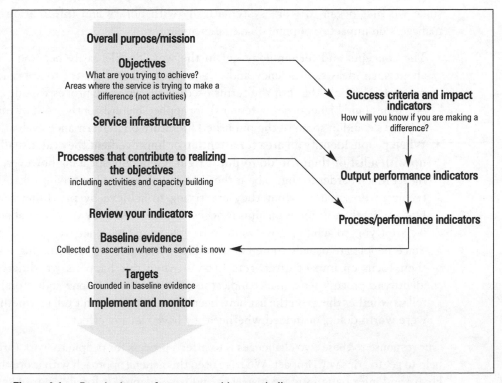

Figure 4.1   *Developing performance and impact indicators*

Each of the steps shown in Figure 4.1 is unpacked in detail in the following chapters. Examples of products at each stage in the process are offered for different types of library service, so the model should be readily adaptable to any project or service management situation.

4.3 Using the model

Managers can use this approach individually, but you will probably gain more if you work through the stages with colleagues. It is possible for a senior management team to work through this model to the data collection stage in a one-day session (assuming that you work in parallel small groups for part of the time), but this is hard going. It may be more productive to tackle the first three stages in a four-hour session and pick up the other steps later.

Six points to watch are:

1 Setting out and agreeing on the aims/objectives and translating some of these into impact indicators will take much longer than you might expect (two to three hours) – if it is done properly.

2 Most if not all library and information services tend to start too far down in the model (at the identification of 'Services that contribute to delivering the aims'). One purpose of this book is to put the impact back into planning. To achieve this it is necessary to spend time on the steps at the top of the model. This is the way to generate impact indicators that will drive your data collection in areas that will provide you with the elusive evidence of impact that is vital to decision making and real service development. Starting too far down results in:

- neglect of *impact* indicators, since these spring from service aims not services delivered
- consulting users and potential users about services (unproblematic and uninformative) rather than about service aims and directions (more contentious and a better basis for *developing* services).

3 We recommend you start at the top of Figure 4.1 (with the overall purpose/mission) and work systematically down the sequence, but move sideways to generate appropriate indicators at each of the three steps shown. The chapters that follow adopt this pattern.

4 It is likely that when you reach the data collection stage you will find that you don't have ready access to baseline information on where you are now. Our experience with various kinds of libraries is that services seldom have baseline impact information, even about areas that they regard as important for development (because such data are not routinely collected to measure the efficiency of the service). If you want to show that a service or initiative is making a difference you need to collect baseline information to show evidence of progress. Planning is central to ensuring that baseline information is available.

5 If you are using this model for development planning, it will be necessary to collect relevant baseline information in order to be able to set sensible targets. You will need to put systems in place that enable you to collect high quality management information more easily (e.g. activity-based costing).

6 If you are looking at improving an aspect of your service, you may choose to get over the problem of 'no baseline information' by putting in the evidence-collection mechanisms and starting to innovate. In this way you will have baseline information at the end of the first period of operation (usually, but not necessarily a year) and will then be able to compare later results against this baseline.

We know from experience that this process helps managers to create appropriate impact indicators and targets anchored in what they are trying to achieve. Some library service managers start the process feeling that impact is too big and amorphous to address but soon realize that they can 'get a handle' on it at key points by carefully relating impact indicators to aims.

The process should help to achieve a balance between the necessary service output and process indicators and targets on the one hand and impact and achievement indicators and targets on the other.

The next few chapters show how this model can be applied in detail to ensure that you can evaluate the impact of your library or information service. However, here are some questions to help you to orientate yourself before you start.

4.4   And the first question is . . .

Unless you have a strong focus on what you already know about yourselves and the services you offer, you are not likely to learn much more. Even before you start looking at the model you should think about why you are interested in service impact and what you hope to gain from having better evidence about your effectiveness. Putting it bluntly, if you aren't sure why you are doing this why not find something more interesting and worthwhile to do?

What kinds of questions do you need to ask yourself before starting the evaluation? Here are four to start with:

1 **Is this evaluation really necessary and, if so, why?** Who is it most necessary or useful for? Is the main purpose to enhance the effectiveness of the service; to demonstrate (and potentially, to increase) value for money; to justify or account for expenditure; or as feedback to identify other areas for development?

2 **Who should do the evaluating?** Who is likely to be able to obtain the co-operation of key informants and library staff? Is it important to get different perspectives when collecting evidence and interpreting results?

3 **What aspects of the service should be evaluated?** Since you are unlikely to have the resources to look at the impact of everything at once, where are you going to start and why?

4 **When should the evaluation be done – or when should it not be done?** You may want to get a picture of the service at all times of year and under all conditions, but you will have to balance this against adding to the pressure by calling for evidence-gathering when the staff are under maximum stress.

Since this whole process is one of development, we suggest that if you are making a start now, you may find it useful to note your answers to these questions, date your answers and file them so that you can look back later and recapture what you thought at the outset and how far you have moved on.

4.5 How do you currently measure your success as a service?

This brings us to another set of questions. How far has your service moved into the area of performance measurement and impact assessment? Please answer the questions below:

1 All library services have some sorts of *service delivery performance indicators* (e.g. issues per number of population served; stock size related to registered users, etc.):

- What do your service delivery indicators concentrate on?
- Do you use the data collected against each of these indicators and, if so, what for? How do they fit into service management, external reporting or the planning cycle? Do you monitor the data closely and act on them or do they mainly serve to show senior managers that you are 'on the case' (on the assumption that if you produce regular performance monitoring data you must be doing your job of watching how well your service is performing)?

2 Most library services use some key *process indicators* linked to delivering services (e.g. 'produce a stock development policy'; 'organize six reading groups'):

- Which processes do you try to monitor?
- What process indicators do you have in place? Do they help you to improve your services? How?

3 Some library services try to measure the *impact of specific services* (e.g. collecting evidence from participants that training provided for users on the internet makes them better 'searchers'):

- Do you collect any evidence of the impact of services? In what areas? How?
- Does this evidence really measure impact?
- Does this evidence help you to improve services? How?

Again, we suggest that you note your answers to these questions now, date your answers and file them to show progress over time.

Example 4.1   A participant comments on the model during its development phase

[The process] has made me think, for example, about the vast (by our standards) sums of money which are being poured into [gathering data as part of a national survey] every year, with the aim of obtaining 'comparable' data. But what exactly are we comparing with – do we not rather tend to breathe a sigh of relief each year at the 'proof' that people still think we are great – 'Please don't close our library'?

Many authorities (our own included) have adopted a policy of each department contributing to every year of Best Value (BV) reviews. Hence we have had to split our service into more or less coherent segments . . . this almost inevitably leads to a focus on activity, rather than aims. There is no opportunity within the BV process to ask fundamental questions about the role of our entire service. And almost inevitably we will end up with [too many performance indicators].

At the same time, and as part of a separate Plan process, we are having to demonstrate how our service contributes to the achievement of corporate aims for lifelong learning, social inclusion . . . but these cross-cutting issues have not been linked explicitly with the BV review programme. Interestingly, the cross-cutting issues which have been identified again are process ones – transport, support services, etc.

Robert Gent

5

Getting things clear: objectives

This chapter focuses on the first stage of the model and explains how to work through it when evaluating the impact of your service. Impact evaluation is essentially about three things:

- **Focus** – being clear about the library's purposes; what you want the service to achieve and for whom (areas of impact)
- **Indicators** – deciding what will tell you that change has happened
- **Evidence** – being able to show that change has occurred.

The first stage of the evaluation process model is about focus.

5.1   Choosing where to get involved

If you are going to be more effective you need to choose how, where and with whom to get involved. Before you can make these decisions you should start with clarifying the impact you want to make – your objectives. However, you need to do this in the real world, so spelling out the objectives should take into account what is achievable. This means making careful choices and adopting clear priorities.

The basic constraint for librarians is having to spend so much time on managing and operating the library infrastructure. This makes it difficult to step back and look critically at what the library is really trying to do: where should you concentrate your efforts? In which areas might you most fruitfully develop your service? The first step in impact evaluation calls for thought about key foci for your service which you can then turn into objectives.

Lack of time is not the only problem; there are also issues of logistics. For example, in *education librarianship* there will always be many teachers and still more students to every librarian. Moreover, both teachers and students will spend much of their time out of the immediate reach of librarians, in the lecture room or classroom. Who should you target and how? Again, *public library services* are being called on to meet more and more externally imposed demands within existing resources. What should take priority and what should be left until later? Other types of libraries will encounter variations on these two constraints.

Responding to both these constraints may well boil down to making choices about where to concentrate on being *efficient* (relying on traditional performance indicators to monitor performance) and where it is important to show yourselves or other people that you are being *proactive and effective*, rather than spreading limited time across too many initiatives. A key consideration is to decide where you can be effective. If you are trying to make an impact it is important to find areas that are ripe for action as well as energetic collaborators – or as educational change guru Michael Fullan (2001) insists 'Go where the energy is'.

Working through the impact evaluation model brings these choices into the open. So, now for the first step in clarifying your focus.

5.2   The mission

In theory, we should probably look to the over-arching purpose or mission statement of the library service to guide our quest for evidence. In practice, although most library services have a mission statement, these are usually bland, often wildly over-optimistic (any statement containing the words 'all users'), and almost invariably too general to be of much help in getting focused. It is not usually worthwhile spending a lot of time refining your mission statement. The main exception here is with a new service or project, where focusing on the mission statement can lead to a useful discussion about what you are really trying to do.

The hard work in evaluating impact begins at the next stage: identifying key areas in which you want your service to make an impact and writing appropriate objectives for each area.

5.3   Where *can* libraries make an impact?

The previous chapter on impact research shows some areas where we know that libraries can make a difference. This research should help to guide any discussion about what your library can achieve and where to focus your activity. For a practitioner perspective on the same question, we don't have to go any further than the aspirations expressed by all the managers who have taken part in our workshops over the past few years. What do they focus on? We summarize for four types of library:

5.3.1   Education libraries

Education librarians in schools through to university libraries tend to concentrate on:

* library use of ICT to support teaching and learning
* basic skills, key skills, information skills and problem-solving skills work involving the library
* collaboration between teachers and library staff; this can be:

— small or large scale (team teaching to resource-based learning projects)
— outside the library
— requiring new roles/skills (not only for library staff).

Although the issues of the moment do tend to change and are likely to be influenced by the political agenda, these general areas for attention have been to the fore for most of the past decade.

5.3.2 Public libraries

Public librarians tend to concentrate on:

- key skills (associated with thinking, learning, reading, ICT and literacy)
- lifelong learning
- social inclusion
- reader development.

Useful additional help is offered by Rebecca Linley and Bob Usherwood (1998), whose work on social impact auditing of two public library services in England concentrates on collecting evidence about the value of the library to the community and its impact on people's lives. They focus on four strands:

- established functions, including culture, education, reading and literacy, information provision and leisure
- social and caring roles, including personal development, community empowerment and learning, local image and social cohesion
- economic impact, including business and employment information, training opportunities and tourism information
- equity between groups and communities, as well as equity of access.

A set of new public library service impact measures has just been introduced in England. These provide a focus by articulating the public library contribution to five government priorities (www.mla.gov.uk/action/framework/framework_04a.asp).

5.3.3 Health libraries

For health librarians, the agenda is partly determined by government or institutional priorities and partly by what is 'hot' in health librarianship. In the first category come:

- meeting the information needs of staff who are directly involved in delivering care to patients
- clinical outreach (ensuring access to and use of best evidence by clinical teams)
- increasing multi-disciplinary use of services.

In the 'hot issues' area come:

- peripatetic trainers/electronic resources training provided by the library service
- systematic ICT training of library staff
- working directly with users to encourage independent learners and an information–seeking culture.

5.3.4 Special libraries

Special libraries obviously vary enormously in their focus. However, in recent workshops two common themes have emerged:

- being a first port of call for managers/researchers in their organization (and beyond in some cases)
- supporting decision making in the organization (by traditional service provision or engaging with knowledge management).

In addition, legal librarians have talked about saving time (and therefore money) for partners.

Step 1   Starting the process
Think about your own library service and decide which key service area or initiative you want to work on now. Use this service area as your focus in working through the impact evaluation model.

5.4   From impact to objectives

5.4.1 Specific and time-limited objectives

When we work with library-service managers, we always start by identifying key areas in which they want their service to make an impact. These areas then provide the focus for generating *specific and time-limited* service objectives.

'Specific', in this context, means being as precise as possible about what you intend to achieve – what advances you expect to make and with which people. We know from our workshops that if managers stick to broad and general objectives, they get into real difficulties when they are asked how they can tell that they are succeeding. This usually entails going back to rewrite the objectives more sharply so that they know where they are trying to get to.

Your definition of 'time-limited' will depend upon whether you are a strategic or operational manager. (Managerial seniority is sometimes delineated by organizations in terms of the length of time over which managers are called upon to plan and deliver services – more senior executives have longer time-scales.) However, the longest realistic operational planning span in most library settings is between one and three years (even where strategic plans are projected over longer periods).

Before focusing on specific objectives, some library services find it helpful to distinguish between user-focused objectives (such as, to enhance lifelong learning opportunities for young people and adults) and internally focused objectives (e.g. to develop the capacity of staff and the organization to learn and improve).

5.4.2 What else do you need to take into account when setting your service objectives?

Objective setting must take account of the wider working context and over-arching organizational priorities. Most library services will be more or less affected by:

- The national agenda as it affects your service – this is self-evident for libraries in central/federal government agencies, and may be important if you are funded by local/state government (especially if your service is heavily influenced by central government direction). In any case the national agenda will affect specific aspects of your work (e.g. through employment legislation). To give one example, UK public libraries have to be seen to address centrally imposed accountability measures (such as the new impact measures for 2005–6 and the service review process). They also have to show that they are in step with specific central government programmes such as the National Literacy Strategy and initiatives (usually brimming with their own jargon) such as those covering social inclusion and lifelong learning. Again, there are national programmes offering direct benefits to public libraries, such as the People's Network (focused on introducing ICT, related staff training and e-development opportunities into public libraries) and other programmes, such as the National Grid for Learning or the University for Industry, which may bring benefits if the opportunities are recognized and seized.
- The local and, especially regional agendas, particularly in countries where development funds are increasingly being made available regionally.
- The interests of other key stakeholders (and potential partners). It is important to be clear who the stakeholders are and how they will be involved in the process. In business and commercial libraries these stakeholders may be easier to identify and consult than in the public sector. When consulting about objectives, it is important to focus on what you are all trying to achieve and how well (that is, on the quality of the collaboration) – otherwise the focus will shift towards activities.

Despite the need to take all these perspectives into account, it is still important to keep your professional judgement in play. The wants expressed by community representatives may not fully reflect community needs. You may have to help people to see what is possible, to open up alternatives and present new ideas. (As a Schools Library Services manager observed: 'It is no good talking to school heads about a quality service if they have no idea what quality looks like.')

5.4.3 Some traps to avoid

Watch out for these three things when writing your objectives:

- Do not set objectives for areas where you have little (or not the main) control over the activities required to meet them.
- Do not simply adopt the objectives of your parent organization. In most organizations it is politically important to take account of and reflect the overall institutional objectives, but it is equally important to ensure that you specify the part that your services should play within that bigger picture – otherwise you will not be able to demonstrate what your service contributed to the whole.
- Try to be realistic about what can be *demonstrably achieved*. It is pointless to set ambitious aims for the service, on the lines of 'the local community will read better' or 'children in schools served will achieve better exam results', if there is no way of establishing whether or not any such impact can be achieved, how to go about it, or whether the library service makes any contribution to achieving any change. Simple cause and effect relationships are difficult to establish in the real world but it should be possible to find objectives with which you can show if you are having any impact – usually by asking people!

If you do fall into one of these traps you are setting yourself up to fail, if other services fail. You will also lose out if success is achieved, because you will not be able to show clearly your part in that success.

Do not be drawn into considering precisely how you will collect your evidence at this stage. Writing objectives is about building a realistic vision of what your service might achieve. Looking at the difficulties of demonstrating achievement too early in the process will inhibit your vision.

5.4.4   . . . and the elephant trap!

The biggest and most common mistake that library managers make at this stage in the impact evaluation process is that they prescribe activities instead of objectives – what they will do to get there rather than what they want to achieve.

Task 5.1

It is not always easy to avoid the elephant trap. Which of the following proposals are impact objectives and which ones are activities?

1   To support managers in carrying out their work effectively and efficiently by providing appropriate information
2   To provide access to ICT-based learning through adult learning sessions
3   To enable students to operate effectively in an e-environment
4   To enable health care staff to find the evidence to develop local care pathways
5   To provide materials appropriate to the needs of ethnic minorities
6   To increase the confidence and competence of socially excluded people in using library resources

7 To develop children as readers

8 To secure the library as a main source of information in conducting research in the field

9 To collaborate with managers in the organization in order to integrate the library into their work

10 To develop the skills of library staff in delivering effective user-education.

(Answers at the end of this chapter)

If you think that you have drifted into specifying activities, ask yourself *why* you are aiming to do the activities – this should take you back to your objectives.

Step 2 Write your objectives

Write between two and four specific and time-limited objectives for your key service area or initiative. Concentrate on what you want to achieve within one to three years, *not* on what you will do to achieve your objectives.

(Some examples of objectives are given in section 5.5.)

5.5 Some examples of objectives

These examples are all based on real objectives generated by library-service managers in different types of library.

5.5.1 Public library services

- to empower individuals and communities to engage in democratic processes
- to support the study needs of young people
- to build individuals' capacity to engage in lifelong learning
- to assist in the reduction of disadvantage and inequality
- to promote and encourage reading across generations
- to contribute to the economic regeneration of the locality
- to sustain community identity and confidence.

5.5.2 Schools library services

- to enrich/extend learning opportunities for all pupils by providing classroom resources
- to support the development of pupils' independent learning skills
- to enable parity of access to resources across schools
- to help extend the range of teaching strategies used to support literacy
- to develop school librarians and school libraries to support reading and learning within schools more effectively

- to promote wider reading
- to support schools' implementation of the Literacy Strategy
- to enable teachers to use a wide range of resources in the classroom more easily
- to promote effective use of ICT within school libraries
- to survive as a business.

Early on in our workshops, library service managers often ask why they should spend so much time writing impact objectives and why we scrutinize the wording of these objectives in such detail. Are we just being pedantic?

In fact, the objectives drive the whole process of impact evaluation. As Peter Brophy (2002) has stressed, no library should think about trying to evaluate its impact before getting its objectives crystal clear. If you use the wrong words at this point you will find it very hard to move on to the next stage, which (as we will show in Chapter 7) involves asking yourself 'How can I tell if we are succeeding in our objective?'. When people hit problems in answering this question, the only way out is to go back and write the objective more precisely.

LAWS OF IMPACT EVALUATION 2
If we are to focus on impact we need to articulate precisely what we are trying to achieve rather than how we will get there.

LAWS OF IMPACT EVALUATION 3
If we don't generate specific and time-limited objectives to help focus on impact, we will end up monitoring efficiency instead.

Answers to Task 5.1

1 is an objective but the last four words have slipped into activity; 2 and 5 are activities; 9 is both an activity and an objective – it should be re-written to focus on the library being integrated into managers' work. If a statement includes 'to provide' this usually heralds an activity.

6

Success criteria and impact indicators: how you know you are making a difference

This chapter guides you through stage two of your quest to evaluate impact: choosing success criteria and using them to write specific impact indicators. The key question at this stage is 'How can I tell if I am making a difference?' or, to put it another way, 'What do I want to be judged on in relation to each of my service objectives?' Designing indicators is one of the most critical steps in the whole process of evaluating impact.

Let us start with two more traps for the unwary.

When we talk about the elephant trap in section 5.4.4, this is because we have seen so many library service managers slide from writing objectives into listing what they expect to do to achieve them. We've come to the conclusion that this happens because the driving motivation for most library managers is to provide as wide a range of services as possible for everyone. Where this is feasible there is no problem, but when resource limitations kick in it is necessary to start asking questions about what works best.

The same problem crops up at this stage, but with the subtle difference that people slide from 'How can I tell if the service is making a difference' to 'How well are we doing this?' As Linley and Usherwood (1998) say:

> Even where people have sought to assess the libraries' performance against goals . . . the emphasis [is] on developing indicators of administrative effectiveness, that is of process.

The second trap to beware of is that it is easy to slide into the problems of collecting the evidence needed to inform your indicators, rather than sorting out the indicators and *then* worrying about the evidence. This leads to library managers shying away from indicators that might be difficult to measure.

Working through this chapter should help you to avoid these traps.

LAWS OF IMPACT EVALUATION 4
When you are thinking about what impact you would like to see, don't inhibit yourself by worrying about how you will gather the evidence – yet!

6.1   Formulating success criteria: getting the balance right

You should now be ready to translate your service objectives into success criteria. If you have written clear objectives, you should be able to answer the questions:

- What sort of changes am I looking for in the people that I want to reach with this service objective?

or

- How can I tell if the parts of the service that are trying to meet this objective are making a difference?

The answers to these questions become your success criteria, which you then turn into impact indicators.

Impact is usually about having an *impact on people*, which creates *change*. What sorts of changes in people are you looking for?

These *changes* may be:

- **affective** (attitudes, perceptions, levels of confidence, satisfaction with the service)
- **behavioural** – people do things differently (e.g. doing something more or less often, asking different types of questions, being more critical or more independent)
- **knowledge-based** (e.g. knowing about key sources of relevant information; knowing what questions different databases can answer)
- **competence-based** – people do things more effectively (e.g. improved search techniques; being able to find appropriate information).

The *people* who may (or may not) change are often your users, but depending on your objectives and how you are carrying them out you may be looking for changes in other people, such as your colleagues, senior managers, teaching staff, local politicians or clients.

Success criteria identify the sorts of changes that you are trying to achieve by addressing your objectives. Impact indicators translate these broad areas into specific pieces of information. The main justification for having the success criteria step in the process before we get stuck into impact indicators is that you are then less likely to lock onto one of the four areas of change above at the expense of the other three.

What we are doing here is similar to what researchers do when they design questionnaires or interview schedules. The first stage in that process is to think of all the *question areas* you want to cover and to decide whether you actually need to cover them all. Beginners tend to jump straight in and start writing *questions*, with the result that they don't usually cover all the important areas and may ask unnecessary questions. Similarly, stepping back and asking 'What criteria will tell me we are being successful?' and 'Which of these will do the job best?' should ensure that you get the balance right.

Examples of success criteria

Objective: Take reading out to targeted community groups
SC 1   More reading (behavioural)
SC 2   Increased book knowledge (knowledge)
SC 3   Develop staff confidence (affective)

Objective: To enhance the user experience of using health literature:
SC 1   Knowing 'what is out there' (knowledge)
SC 2   Increased user satisfaction (affective)
SC 3   Improved ability to do their job (competence)

Step 3   Write success criteria
Choose two of the service objectives that you wrote earlier (section 5.4.4). Write two or three success criteria for each one. Make sure that you focus on changes in people.

6.2   What is an impact indicator?

In the world of performance management that we occupy, the word 'indicator' is freely bandied about. What is an indicator and how can it help us to evaluate impact? An indicator is a piece of information that indicates something useful to you. Indicators are not produced or used in a vacuum. They are tied to your service objectives. They must be seen in the context of what you are trying to do.

Indicators can only give you clues about the difference you are making. It is extremely difficult to evaluate the actual impact of any service. Human beings are complex and are affected in many subtle ways by each experience. Impact indicators are usually surrogates for impact: pieces of information that provide good clues, telling part of the story. Your challenge is to design the strongest surrogates possible. For example, assume that your service is trying to encourage enthusiasm for books and reading. You may decide to monitor loan levels, but this is a weak surrogate for the impact that you are trying to record. Loans might increase for a number of reasons. A much stronger surrogate, and therefore a better indicator, is users' attitudes towards books – are they more positive as a result of your work?

6.3   What do good indicators look like?

Much has been written during the past 20 years about designing good indicators (for example, Kaplan and Norton, 1992; Fitz-Gibbon, 1996; Woodcock, 1998). Lists of their characteristics abound. Education, in particular, has engaged in many debates about what makes a good indicator.

Example 6.1   Avoid too many indicators and still focus on what really matters: looking at schools

Here is an example from an education workshop for school heads and advisers that we both attended some years ago.

A leading university professor began by saying that he only needs three pieces of information about a school to know how good it is – examination results, teacher absence rates and levels of truancy (unauthorized absence by students). Not surprisingly this pronouncement was greeted with shock and horror. However, he maintained his position, arguing that these three indicators illuminate the impact of the school on pupils and teachers.

An education inspector at the same workshop replied that he wants four indicators to judge the quality of education and a school's effectiveness: academic progress, pupil satisfaction, positive pupil–teacher relationships and instances of excellence within the learning process. (Neither speaker suggested looking at the number of classes taught, levels of expenditure, staffing levels, resources per pupil or anything else – the educational equivalent of what many library services do.)

They tied their indicators firmly into what the schools should be trying to achieve: progress in pupil learning, a supportive environment for pupils and teachers, and engaging with all pupils in the school.

This exchange illustrates some of the most important factors to bear in mind when you are creating good indicators. Indicators should be:

- **directly linked to what you are trying to achieve**. The key areas in which you are trying to make a difference (relevant to accepted and valued organizational goals). This is why we give so much attention to articulating objectives before getting any further into evaluating impact.
- **clear and understandable**. Check them with colleagues at all levels.
- **generally accepted as reasonable and fair**. You need to agree that the indicators really do tell you about the impact of your service. Are they measuring something over which you have little control (hardly fair), something that does not tell the whole story of what you are achieving, or things of secondary importance in the eyes of your staff or managers? Are they up-to-date? You may be doing invaluable online support work for managers in your organization but this may result in declining use of your physical space or reference material. Do your indicators reflect such changes? (There is always likely to be some discussion about how fair your chosen indicators are.)
- **valid** (evaluate what they say they are evaluating). This is more difficult than it seems – for example, a public library registers a surge in use after it runs an awareness-raising programme. It is delighted at this impact until someone notices that most of the new users are in the 18–21 age group, and the local college has just closed the site library nearest to that public library.

- **informative, providing significant information.** They should illuminate your successes, highlight changes/trends and throw up warning signs.
- **as few in number as possible**. They should cover the most significant parts of the service (what really matters). The question to ask is 'What are the most important changes that you are trying to achieve?' However, you also need to make sure that the indicators are balanced. You don't want to choose a very small number of indicators and then find that they pull your attention and even your whole service in the wrong direction (more about this below).

An important issue here is how many impact indicators you really need and how to choose the key areas. If you have consulted over your objectives and prioritized them, it is reasonable to confine your impact indicators to the priority areas in which you are trying to make a noticeable difference and to rely on traditional process and output performance indicators (see sections 7.4 and 7.5) to monitor other areas.

6.4   What makes a poor indicator?

There are several ways in which indicators can fail to do their job. They can be:

- **corruptible** – easily used to create a false impression. For example, library managers assure us that they could massage or selectively use their loan statistics to show a range of desired outcomes, from demonstrating the excellent job they are doing to indicating problems in the hope of getting more resources!
- **corrupting** – provide an incentive to do disruptive or counter-productive actions; such as when a police force introduces 'time taken to answer phone calls' as an indicator of effectiveness, resulting in a discussion with a distressed robbery victim being broken off to answer the next call! It is also a common occurrence on London trains for all travellers to be turned off at an intermediate station so that the train can run through to the end of the line without further stops – the indicator is 'Proportion of trains that arrive on time'! Your indicators should always encourage positive service.

   In libraries, corrupting indicators might focus on one or two aspects of the service to the detriment of others. To avoid this, remember that your indicators should reflect the competing priorities that all services have to struggle with.
- **inflexible** and unable to reflect diversity and change in your services – how many libraries that are now offering interesting ICT-based services are evaluating them actively to show how their services are changing?

6.5   Some issues to consider before you start writing indicators

- You should focus impact indicators on changes that you are deliberately setting out to achieve and at which you have targeted resources. These changes should be clear from your service objectives.
- It should be possible to find two or three indicators of impact in relation to each objective. Sometimes the same impact indicator can be used for more than one objective.

- Indicators are provisional. It is very rare to get indicators completely right at the first attempt. We don't usually know enough at the outset about the complex relationships between different factors and different elements of any service. The first time you work through the measuring impact process you may find that some indicators do not tell you what you really need to know while others distract you from the real issues. Change them.
- Don't be distracted by *how* you will gather the necessary evidence. It is important to resist the normal managerial tendency to consider the 'what' and 'how' questions together. If you lose the distinction, you will probably slide into output indicators (e.g. quantity of loans to socially disadvantaged groups) because these are easier to collect. Once you decide that it is important to assess an area of impact you will probably be able to find some way of gathering evidence. (We look at data collection in Chapter 9.)
- You may have to revisit your objectives when you start to look for appropriate indicators. For example, one service abandons its aim of 'promoting literacy' when service managers consider how much direct effect they can have. Instead, they opt for 'supporting literacy through partner organizations' and the impact indicators flow more naturally.
- It may be easier to assess impact at some levels than at others. For example, if a schools' library service provides training and advice for teachers from several schools it should be possible to collect some evidence of any change in their awareness and behaviour; it will be much harder to demonstrate any impact on pupils.
- Some services group their indicators by the strategic, operational or service level at which they are applied (e.g. specific service points; organization-wide). You may like to use this as a checking mechanism to ensure that all the indicators are not clustered at one level – after you have identified your indicators.
- It is difficult to *measure* some tangible benefits that libraries can bring (e.g. personal development, community empowerment, quality of pupil work). However, indicators of impact do not have to be quantitative and therefore easily measured. Qualitative indicators (e.g. Do members of socially excluded groups feel more able to contribute their ideas to library managers?) can be equally valid.

Please don't forget that whatever indicators you choose, professional judgement still matters!

6.6   **Writing indicators**

Writing indicators requires effort: they should be unambiguous – make it clear what evidence you need to collect to see how you are doing – and you should be able to apply them in a sustainable manner so that by collecting evidence year-on-year you can see any trends.

We now discuss some of the choices you have about the form of the indicators that you write.

6.6.1 Different forms of indicators

People write indicators in different ways. This may be based on the accepted approach in an organization, 'how they are always written'; or they may follow guidelines; or someone may attend a course where a certain approach is used. Unless you are constrained by organizational rules, think carefully about the type of indicators that you will find it easiest to work with. Which of the formats below do you prefer? Which will you find easiest to write? Which format seems the clearest?

6.6.2 Indicators as questions

You can find this approach in our school library self-evaluation materials produced for the English Department for Education and Skills (Streatfield and Markless, 2004). For instance, in looking at the objective of improving the standard of pupils reading, the indicators chosen are:

- Do pupils read a wide range of challenging material?
- Do pupils respond imaginatively to what they have read?
- Do pupils enjoy reading?
- Do pupils show progression in their reading, extending the range and level of material chosen over time?

Questions like these are clear: they focus on important areas of impact for any reading programme; they point you towards collecting particular information; and they can be used over time to signal trends.

6.6.3 Indicators as statements

Indicators written as short statements are common in library plans. An example is the Their Reading Futures website (www.theirreadingfutures.org.uk), which offers the following indicators of success for promoting reading among young people, in the form of brief statements:

1 Young people read more widely.
2 Young people become more confident about themselves as readers.
3 Young people have more positive attitudes towards reading.
4 Young people and families have an increased sense of belonging to the community through reading and reading activities.
5 Through reading and reading activities young people are inspired to engage in creative activities.

6.6.4 Indicators as quantities

Many managers are obsessed with numbers. This is partly due to pressure from government departments and other influential bodies that hold the purse strings, and partly because many managers think that the only valid evidence is quantitative. Library-service managers should be trying to re-educate senior staff who exhibit this type of tunnel vision. However, there is of course a place for some numbers in the evaluation of impact and it is possible to write indicators in quantitative terms. You could rewrite any of the indicators given in sections 6.6.2 or 6.6.3 above as numbers or proportions (e.g. 'the proportion of pupils who enjoy reading', or 'the percentage of young people who read more widely').

Numbers can only tell you a limited amount. It may be more important to find out about the nature and magnitude of the changes that have occurred rather than just how many people were involved. Quantitative indicators can also pull you into thinking about the numbers too early in the process of evaluating impact. When you come to think about setting targets (Chapter 10) you will inevitably be drawn into enumerating your targets. At this earlier stage, when you are thinking about indicators for evaluating impact, it is often more productive to consider in broad terms the types of information that tell you what difference you are making; these may or may not be numerical.

LAWS OF IMPACT EVALUATION 5

Beware of formulating too many quantitative indicators. This can lead you to concentrate too heavily on the statistical side of your impact – numbers never tell the whole story.

Step 4   What kind of indicators?

You now need to decide what your impact indicators will look like. For example, which of the following do you prefer?

- The proportion of managers who use the library as a first port of call when needing information about their work.
- Managers use the library as a first port of call when needing information about their work.
- Do managers use the library as a first port of call when needing information about their work?

You can, of course, switch between or vary your formats, as long as you retain clarity.

6.7   Writing your own impact indicators

You have already formulated some success criteria linked to two of your service objectives. You can now use these to write your impact indicators. At this stage you are looking at the sort of changes that you want to achieve (success criteria) and deciding what specific pieces of information will enable you to judge whether you are making that difference. It is usual to write between two and four indicators for each of your objectives.

Later on, when you have written a full set of impact indicators that cover all of your service objectives you should review them as a package. This gives you the chance to get rid of any overlap and duplication, so that you end up with the smallest set of indicators that still demonstrate your success.

Step 5   Write impact indicators

Revisit the two service objectives and associated success criteria that you have already produced. Use the success criteria to help you to write impact indicators for each of the two service objectives.

Sections 6.8 and 6.9 should help you with this activity. You may prefer to do the task first and then use the information to check or amend your indicators. If you prefer to have all the information at your disposal before you begin, read to the end of section 6.9 before doing the task.

6.8   Getting the words right

Clarity is one of the most important characteristics of a good indicator. Your indicators tell you what evidence you need to collect to see if you are achieving your service objectives. They also establish what you will be judged on. So, your indicators need to be precisely worded to make sure that you do not set yourself up to fail. Our concern with getting the words right is not born out of a desire to be pedantic. It arises from our experience of running workshops for practitioners and from our development work with library senior management teams engaging in evaluating their own service impact. We often spend time with library staff going through their indicators and 'fine tuning' them. How well this time is spent will become evident at the next stage when you begin to plan data collection.

Here are some examples of this fine-tuning (drawn from our workshops), along with our reasons for making the suggested changes.

Example 6.1 Impact indicators for a special library

The library staff drew up the following lists of impact indicators for two of their key service objectives.

Objective 1:   To support managers carrying out their work with appropriate information

1 Managers make more challenging demands of the information service.
2 More managers use the service as a first port-of-call when seeking information (directly or indirectly).
3 More managers know about the specialist information services provided by the library.
4 More managers make appropriate use of the specialist information services provided by the library.

Objective 2:   To secure the library as a main source of information in conducting research in the field

1 Researchers make regular use of the research resources of the library (directly and indirectly).
2 Researchers make written acknowledgement of the library in their published works.
3 Researchers recommend the library to other potential users.
4 Users make more challenging demands on the services of the library when conducting their research.

Activity

What do you think of the indicators in Example 6.1?
Would you make any changes?
If so, what changes and why?

Try to answer these questions before you look at our comments below.

6.8.1   Commentary on Example 6.1

Objective 1

The first indicator is fine. It focuses on a specific change in behaviour by the group identified in the objective. It should give useful information about the nature of the help that the library service is providing.

Indicators 2, 3 and 4 need some attention. All of them focus on whether the service is having an impact on managers. They all appear to identify significant elements of behaviour and they all lead the service manager towards gathering particular types of evidence. The problem is in the use of the word 'more' at the beginning of each of the indicators. An indicator should keep the options open rather than lead you towards a predetermined outcome. You do not know in advance whether more or fewer managers will make appropriate use of the service. It is probably better to say 'Managers make appropriate use . . .' or 'Managers know about . . .' if only to avoid the temptation of putting your foot on the scales by concentrating on indicators in areas where you know you can show an improvement. As you collect data over time you will be able to see whether more people are behaving as you would want. (The neutral position we are suggesting here will be abandoned when you come to set impact targets at the next stage. As we will show in Chapter 10, that is why targets can corrupt the service they are trying to evaluate.)

Objective 2

The first three indicators should work. However, when we discussed the fourth indicator with the library staff, they decided that although it might be a good indicator of effective use of the library, it would not give them clear information about whether they are achieving this particular objective of securing the library as a main source of research information in the field. They changed it to:

4 Researchers use the library as a first port-of-call when seeking information.

Example 6.2 Impact indicators for a college library

Objective 1:   To enable students to operate effectively in an e-environment
1 Proportion of students using the e-resources.
2 More efficient and successful searching by a wider range of students.
3 Students are confident in dealing with e-resources.
4 Students are producing better quality work.

Objective 2:   To develop students' ability to find and use appropriate information
1 Students' engagement with their library-based assignments (motivation, interest).
2 Range of resources used by students for their work.
3 Student questions in the library are less basic and more focused.
4 Students are producing better quality work.
5 Students are confident in carrying out their assignments.

Activity
What do you think of the indicators in Example 6.2?
Would you make any changes?
If so, what changes and why?

Try to answer these questions before you look at our comments below.

6.8.2   Commentary on Example 6.2

Objective 1

The first three indicators taken together appear appropriate and manageable, although the first one is a weak surrogate for impact. The library staff decided to keep it in because they hoped to show senior management that more students were being attracted to e-resources. The fourth indicator raised a problem. It is difficult to make a direct link between enabling students to operate effectively in an e-environment and the general quality of their work (although you might like to try). After discussion, the library staff replaced this indicator with two others:

4 Students cite e-resources in their assignments.
5 Students are able to use the web independently to access appropriate material.

They then decided to remove indicator 2 about efficient and successful searching (remembering the cardinal rule about using as few indicators as possible), because it was subsumed in the new indicator 5. When the librarians gather data about students' use of the web they will be able to see the range of students who can use it effectively and whether this range is broadening over time. By the end of our discussion there were still four indicators attached to Objective 1, but they were different:

Objective 1:   To enable students to operate effectively in an e-environment
Revised indicators:

1 Proportion of students using the e-resources.
2 Students are confident in dealing with e-resources.
3 Students cite e-resources in their assignments.
4 Students are able to use the web independently to access appropriate material.

Objective 2

Again, the first three indicators work. However, indicator 4 raises the same problem as in the previous example – over-extending the reach of the library. In this case they changed it to:

4 Students know about a range of appropriate information sources.

The last indicator also appears a step too far. Rather than expect information-skills teaching to produce students who are confident throughout the process of carrying out their assignments, they decide to limit their aspirations to:

5 Students are confident in finding appropriate material for their assignments.

6.9   Using frameworks to help you choose appropriate indicators

Although your indicators should flow from your own service objectives, there is no need to start the writing process from scratch. You can use existing frameworks to point you in the right direction and give you some useful ideas. Don't follow them slavishly: consult them to see if they contain material that can be adapted to reflect what you want to achieve. Be careful that any model or framework that you use is looking at impact and not only at process (activities you should engage in). In practice, indicators in these frameworks are often a mix of impact and process. Try labelling them as P (process) or I (impact) so that you can see which ones you might borrow.

6.9.1 Framework 1: Inspiring Learning for All

The Inspiring Learning for All framework is the jewel in the crown of the UK Museums, Libraries and Archives Council. It aims to describe 'what an accessible and inclusive museum, archive or library which stimulates and supports learning looks like'. The focus of this framework is on *informal learning* stimulated by public libraries (as well as museums and archives) and it tries to help service managers to:

- Find out what the people that use your services learn
- Assess how well you are achieving best practice in supporting learning
- Improve what you do.

To help achieve these aims, Inspiring Learning for All identifies a set of fairly traditional generic learning outcomes (in our terms, success criteria) which replicate the four areas of change outlined in section 6.1 above:

- knowledge and understanding (our 'knowledge-based')
- skills (our 'competence-based')
- attitudes and values (our 'affective')
- enjoyment, inspiration, creativity (again, our 'affective')
- activity, behaviour and progression (our 'behavioural').

These success areas are then unpacked into more specific success criteria. For example, 'knowledge and understanding' is broken down into 'knowing about something', and this in turn is categorized as:

- learning facts or information which can be:
  — subject-specific
  — interdisciplinary/thematic
  — about libraries
  — about myself, my family, my community, the wider world
- making sense of something
- deepening understanding
- learning how libraries operate
- giving specific information – naming things, people or places
- making links and relationships between things
- using prior knowledge in new ways.

Inspiring Learning for All also identifies what it calls 'learning outcomes for users'. Most of these can be developed into impact indicators. At the moment, we think that they are not specific enough to enable a clear enough focus on impact and on gathering evidence. Some examples are:

- People enjoy themselves and are enriched and inspired by the experience.
- People use the services and facilities to develop their knowledge and understanding.
- People develop skills as a result of using libraries.

- People become more self-confident, questioning, motivated and open to others' perspectives.
- People decide to do something different in their lives.

They also identify some 'outcomes for the . . . library', which are more specific and can be used as impact indicators:

- A broader range of people use the . . . library.
- New learning opportunities are created as a result of partnerships.
- Staff, volunteers and members of governing bodies are effective advocates for learning.
- People who work in and for the organization are continuously learning and developing their practice.

The Inspiring Learning for All framework and a range of support materials can be found at www.inspiringlearningforall.gov.uk.

We will return to this framework when we look at development planning at the end of Chapter 10.

6.9.2   Framework 2: the Fitz-Gibbon model

Carol Fitz-Gibbon and Susan Kochan (2000) offer a useful way of focusing on impact indicators that works for education libraries, although their focus is on helping schools to improve. In introducing these areas they recognize the danger of confining impact (their 'outcomes') evaluation to what is formally learnt, and ask:

> how do we move beyond the cognitive to a comprehensive list of important and valued outcomes? In attempting to produce a list of education outcomes, we can take the approach of considering the desired sequence of events in the education of a [student], then identify the logical outcomes related to each step in the sequence. The [student] should:
>
> - enrol at the [college/university] and then attend
> - achieve
> - develop desirable attitudes
> - develop desirable skills
> - have a good quality of life while in the [college]; and
> - then progress appropriately onwards.

They then translate this series of events into impact indicators. We have modified these to fit school, college or university library contexts. Examples of impact indicators include:

- **Flow** (enrol at and attend):
  - — The proportion of students who are formally introduced to the library and then use it compared with those who are not 'induced'. (If this proportion can be calculated it gives an indication of the effect of induction and its contribution to flow.)
  - — Nature of enquiries/requests for help from inducted versus non-inducted students.
- **Cognitive outcomes** (achieve)
  One important direct way for the library to affect student learning is through aspects of the student assignment – if library staff make a specific input to assignment preparation:
  - — the inclusion and adequacy of any bibliography
  - — the number and range of sources cited
  - — how the sources are presented and used
  - — teacher views of the overall quality of the work compared with that of people who had not been prepared for their assignment by library staff (or possibly of non-library users).
- **Affective outcomes** (desirable attitudes)
  - — levels of student confidence in using the library
  - — levels of self-esteem
  - — positive student views of library staff
  - — positive student perceptions of the value and relevance of library services
  - — readiness of students to use a range of resources.
- **Skills**
  - — students demonstrate information literacy skills (sometimes called information literacy scaffolds)
  - — students use information literacy strategies effectively and efficiently
  - — students show independence when doing research.
- **Quality of life**
  - — students form positive relationships with library staff
  - — students show motivation
  - — students engage in the learning process
  - — students' learning is enriched (especially minority groups in terms of ability, culture, language etc.).
- **Long term outcomes** (progression)
  - — former students use libraries/information services over time
  - — former students recognize continued benefits from their information literacy training when they were students.

6.9.3 Framework 3: looking at the audience

You may find it useful to think about the different target audiences you want to affect. For example:

- For **public library services** these might include: different sorts of individuals (e.g. children, teenagers, parents and children together, single parents and their children, old people, unemployed people), local groups and associations, local ethnic communities, the local authority and local businesses.
- For **health library services** these could include: health managers, clinicians, students, patients, staff in allied professions and hospital workers following courses.

It is worth keeping an eye out for innovations in impact work. For example, the Museums, Libraries and Archives Council in the UK recently launched a toolkit of resources for public library staff to evaluate the long-term impact of IT-based services on users (Brophy and Craven, 2004).

Step 6   Test the indicators
Revisit the impact indicators that you have written for two of your service objectives. Show them to two colleagues and ask:

- Are they clear?
- Will they tell me if I am achieving my objectives?
- Are they reasonable things for me to achieve? (Am I reaching too far?)

6.10   Some indicators
Finally, here are some real examples of impact indicators, tied into service objectives. These were all generated by library-service managers and may help you now and in the future when you write impact indicators. You may find useful indicators among those produced by people working in other library sectors, which can be readily adapted. For example, you could replace 'clinicians' with solicitors, managers or researchers; and 'socially excluded groups' with any minority group of users.

Example 6.3   Impact indicators for health libraries

Objective 1:   More empowered and effective users
1 Users locate relevant material and apply it in practice.
2 Users ask more sophisticated questions.
3 More confident users.

Objective 2:   A literature search service that positively contributes to patient care
1 Proportion of clinicians reporting that the search contributes to patient care.
2 Proportion of clinicians reporting that previously unknown evidence has been identified.
3 Proportion of clinicians reporting that the service is useful.

Objective 3: Provision of an effective current literature search process

1 Proportion of clinicians who follow up the search and ask for articles.
2 Proportion of searches focused in the wrong area.
3 Proportion of clinicians reporting that the process is straightforward.

Objective 4: To support healthcare staff in finding the evidence to develop local care pathways

1 Awareness of the evidence base; 'what is out there' and 'where to find it'.
2 Trainees' confidence in identifying the evidence to underpin the construction of a 'local care pathway'.
3 Trainees' effectiveness in identifying the evidence to underpin the construction of a local care pathway.

Objective 5: Targeted staff making more effective use of evidence-based information in clinical practice

1 Staff offer better-expressed clinical questions.
2 Staff offer more challenging clinical questions.
3 Staff more competent in appraising evidence.
4 Evidence base being used by targeted staff.

[Would it be better to express 1 to 3 in neutral impact terms?]

Example 6.4 Impact indicators for public libraries

Objective 1: To ensure access to ICT for people with sensory and mobility impairments

1 Proportion of people with sensory and mobility impairments using libraries.
2 Levels of competence and confidence in using ICT.
3 Levels of interest in e-learning opportunities.

Objective 2: To ensure staff awareness and competence in relation to aspects of social inclusion

1 Staff knowledge about engaging with people who are socially excluded.
2 Staff taking a more proactive approach to meeting customer needs.
3 Staff confidence in engaging with people who are socially excluded.
4 Do people who are socially excluded perceive that they are treated equally and have equal access to resources?

Objective 3: Enhanced public library role in lifelong learning

1 Levels of knowledge of provision.
2 Levels of use of a variety of relevant services.
3 Increased valuing of the service by 'silver surfers'.

4 Proportion of people not previously taking up learning opportunities who are using ICT in the library to participate in lifelong learning

Objective 4:   Identified needs of targeted communities are better met by library services

1 Are people from ethnic communities aware of free access to libraries and their entitlement to services?
2 Are people from ethnic communities able to utilize the available services?
3 Do ethnic communities show more confidence in contributing their views to service development within cultural constraints?

Example 6.5 Impact indicators for schools library services (regional services supporting school libraries and librarians)

Objective 1:   Enhance teachers' use of resources in the classroom
1 Range of resources used by teachers during literacy/numeracy lessons.
2 Level of teacher awareness of curriculum-related resources.
3 Level of teacher awareness of strategies for using non-fiction resources in the classroom.

Objective 2:   Enable wider reading by pupils
1 Reduced dependence on reading schemes or on a limited range of authors.
2 Ability of schools to provide appropriate reading material to pupils with special educational needs or ethnic minority pupils.
3 Ability of pupils to find books in school that meet their interests and needs.

Example 6.6 Impact indicators for school libraries

Objective 1:   To develop information literate students
1 More positive attitudes to learning.
2 Capacity to manage difficult learning tasks.
3 Enhanced self-esteem and confidence as learner.
4 Greater motivation.
5 Greater collaboration among peers.

7

Making things happen: activities and process indicators

Here we look at translating objectives into action. It is the most straightforward and least demanding stage of the process for most libraries. We know from our workshops that once people have a clear idea of what they are trying to achieve it is usually fairly easy to think of a variety of ways to get there. Then, when you have decided on what to do, finding ways of telling whether you have done them (process indicators) is not usually very challenging.

7.1 Why activities? Why now?

We have taken up a lot of space in the last few chapters warning you of the dangers of getting sidetracked when you are trying to evaluate your impact by looking at what you do (activities and processes), rather than concentrating on what difference you make. Why are we moving the goalposts now? Activities do matter: you need to think about them and keep them under review. That is why we have written this chapter. However, if you want this stage in the process to support the evaluation of your impact, you need to get the timing and the focus right.

7.1.1 Timing

You should leave any consideration of activities and processes until *after* you have completed your initial work on objectives and impact indicators. We have seen what happens to impact evaluation when library managers get caught up with questions about service delivery, allocation of resources, allocating staff time and prioritizing among a wide range of activities. Attention slips away from impact with the result that planning once again focuses around provision. For example, the UK public library Annual Library Plans are replete with specific processes and actions aimed at keeping the services going, enhancing the library infrastructure and activity-building. These processes very much reflect the hands-on operationally focused approach of many library managers. We are not saying that such concerns are not important, just that they need to wait until now, after you clarify what you want to achieve and how you will know you are being successful.

7.1.2 Focus

The danger when considering activities and processes is that you might record everything that you are doing in the general area covered by your objectives. We recommend that you tie activities into the objectives, specifically linking a set of actions to each impact objective. It is not helpful to generate a raft of activities that outline the totality of what you do to achieve your goals. Focus is vital if you want to use any evidence gathered about your impact as the basis for service development. If you want to sustain or increase your effectiveness in a particular area of work or with a particular group of users, you need to know what you did to make a difference in the first place. You are then in a position to decide whether you can do different things, alter the balance between activities or take an entirely different route to your goal. You therefore need to review regularly the activities related to each impact objective in the light of the data you collect about how successfully you are meeting that objective.

7.2   Identify activities

Librarians are good at identifying activities – it is a fairly automatic part of library planning.

If you are working through this evaluation process, you have already formulated and checked your service objectives. It should not take you long to decide on the main activities you need to meet them. Some library services differentiate between various types of processes and activities. For example, they separate out internal business processes, continuous improvement actions and financial actions. If you adopt this approach it may be easier to check that you have included all the main elements of what you need to do to make a difference.

When you identify the activities needed to meet a particular objective, try to strip your thinking of any pre-conceptions. Try not to assume that any of your services or interventions should continue automatically. Examine them all critically. Look at each objective carefully and ask what you really need to do to achieve it. Do you need to put any additional services in place? Do you need to change your whole approach? (In public libraries in England this critical examination has been formalized into a national Best Value review process.) You may want to 'brainstorm' other ways of meeting your objectives (or 'get out of the box' in the current management jargon). If you try this, make sure that you get away from the constraining presence of your normal workplace and remember that, in the words of a Swedish group facilitator, 'When you are brainstorming, 50% of your ideas should be silly ideas' or, rather, ideas that may not look realistic at the outset.

Step 7   Turn objectives into actions
Choose two of your objectives and identify the key activities required to meet them successfully.

Example 7.1   Activities that contribute to realizing impact objectives

Specialist information services
Objective: To enhance the quality of policy decision-making by education officers in local government

Activities

1 Encourage education officers to contribute their policy and management documents to the information exchange, concentrating on new initiatives and 'good practice'.
2 Circulate sets of abstracts of these documents to all the education officers.
3 Provide copies of these documents to the education officers on request.
4 Encourage recipients to contact the original donors to find out more about the decision-making context.

School libraries

Objective: To enhance the quality of pupils' reading

Activities

1 Actively promote reading for enjoyment (author events; reading games; newsletters; themed displays outside the library).
2 Organize continuing professional development for teaching staff (training workshops).
3 Organize a bookclub providing positive feedback to pupils on their reading.
4 Collaborate with the school's literacy co-ordinator to plan and deliver lessons.
5 Set up special projects to encourage 13-year-old boys to read.
6 Involve pupils in library stock selection.

7.3   Review the activities

When you have identified the activities that relate to each of your objectives, you should review them as a whole. You will probably find that a number of activities appear more than once, linked to different objectives. At this stage it is useful to note the duplication but to leave it in place. When you reach the action planning stage (see Chapter 10) you can make sure that you are not doing the same thing three times.

7.4   Process indicators

Once you have decided what steps or actions to take you should find it relatively easy to choose the process indicators that will tell you whether you are doing them. Process indicators (sometimes referred to rather confusingly as 'performance indicators') are readily identifiable as the sorts of indicator that can be 'ticked off the list when you've done them'. You use process indicators to monitor your activities, to check whether you are on course or whether you have been sidetracked or slowed down. Not surprisingly, as well as being full of intended activities, library plans are replete with rafts of process indicators that tell if you are doing them; these are the two 'strong areas' of library service planning.

Process indicators are fairly easy to generate and to collect evidence about. Unfortunately, they do not necessarily tell you if you are meeting the impact objectives that led you to carry out the activity in the first place. For example, if you decide that a round of executive briefings is necessary to ensure that managers make more effective use of the service, your process indicator might be 'the number of briefing sessions that are held'. But this won't tell you whether the messages are getting home and whether they are leading to changes in the behaviour of the managers. (That is why we wrote this book.)

Since each objective is delivered through its own set of activities, every objective will trail a set of process indicators in its wake as well as the impact indicators you have already generated.

Example 7.2 Process indicators

Schools library services
Objective: Broadening the scope of reading material used by pupils
Process indicators:

- a range of fiction and non-fiction books provided to all member primary schools
- the number of workshops run for secondary school teachers on integrating books into the curriculum
- teachers given advice about choosing and buying books (e.g. what motivates teenage boys)
- the proportion of primary schools in which reading promotion events have been organized
- the proportion of secondary schools provided with multimedia resources to motivate pupils
- the number of contributions made to workshops for teachers run by local government inspectors
- reading lists to support the National Literacy Strategy sent to all schools.

Specialist information services
Objective: To enhance the quality of policy decision-making by education officers in local government
Process indicators:

- range of policy and management documents contributed
- number of sets of abstracts of documents sent to education officers
- number of copies of documents requested
- number of copies of documents supplied
- number of enquiries referred to original donors.

When you are thinking about activities and how to tell whether you are doing them (performance), there are usually two areas to focus on: what you are doing (processes) and what level of activity this generates (outputs). (We have already said that outputs provide a measure of efficiency and are traditionally measured quantitatively, e.g.

number of services provided and number of people provided for, or numbers of books issued.) These translate into process indicators and output indicators. You may also like to focus on the resources that you are putting into the activities (input indicators), but these usually come into play only when they are combined with other measures as output indicators, as we show below. Don't worry too much about these distinctions. These are all indicators about performance.

7.5   Output indicators

Output (sometimes called service) indicators focus on the amount of business or traffic produced by your chosen activity. In general, in telling you what you need to know about whether things are happening and whether they make a difference, these indicators are likely to be less useful than either impact or process indicators – but they do have a place. Output indicators are usually created by bringing together *two or more measures* to say something about the level of delivery of the particular service you are looking at. For example, you can combine an input measure (such as number of books purchased) and an output measure (such as number of loans) to produce an indicator of intensity of new stock use. Equally, you can combine process indicators and output measures. For example, you can link the number of book promotion events held at a library (process) to prior and subsequent loans by that library (output). This gives an output indicator of sorts relating to the effects of the events on library loans, but it is a weak one. There are several other factors that may have affected loans. A stronger output indicator is possible if you can link prior and subsequent loans to the actual people who participated in the promotional events. (Even then, of course, you don't know whether people read the books they borrow, let alone whether reading them has any effect on them.)

The distinction between process indicators and output indicators is not always clear cut, so don't spend too much time on discriminating between them. Try to avoid the perennial library management trap of collecting too many output indicators instead of looking at impact.

Example 7.3   Output indicators

Public library services

- net expenditure on the service per head of population
- net expenditure per library visit or telephone enquiry
- number of library visits per square metre of accommodation
- numbers attending training events organized by public libraries
- numbers of PCs accessible per 100,000 of population
- proportion of stock on loan from each service point.

Schools library services

- proportion of stock on loan to each secondary school
- numbers of teachers or librarians attending in-service training events delivered by SLS staff
- number of 'hits' on various parts of the SLS website
- number of schools that have availed themselves of the SLS advisory service.

7.6 Process and output indicators: things to watch

In section 6.3 we give you a list of the characteristics of good indicators as well as what to avoid when writing them. You might want to revisit our advice at this point, since it applies just as much to process and output indicators as to impact indicators. However, because process and output indicators are easier to write, you will usually encounter fewer problems. It is still worth taking time to ensure that your indicators are:

- **informative** (giving reassurance that processes are working or warning signs if they are not)
- **able to be changed** (provisional; since not all performance indicators will turn out to be useful)
- **reliable** (telling you something useful each time that they are checked)
- **accessible and understandable** to all those likely to be affected by using them (staff, managers and people to whom the service is accountable)
- **acceptable** (seen to be fair; checkable)
- **cost-effective** (the additional costs of collecting data should not outweigh the benefits of using them. Can you use existing systems or data routinely collected by someone else?)

Of course, they should also be as few in number as possible.

7.7 The 'reach' of the service

We suggest in section 7.5 that output indicators are, in general, less informative than process or impact indicators. We also pointed out earlier that the classic 'input – process – output – outcomes' model for performance measurement tends to break down when we aggregate outputs to arrive at the outcomes (unlike the engineering process field where doing this usually works).

There is one significant exception to this rule – if you are looking broadly enough at a library service, or if you are looking at a number of library services, you can aggregate some outputs to provide useful information in relation to the 'reach' of the service. The 'reach' of the service is calculated by looking at your potential clientele and relating this to the actual number of service users. You can also refine this process to look at particular types of potential and actual users, compare the 'reach' of particular parts of your service, or look at the 'reach' in different geographical locations.

National targets for library services tend to be expressed in terms of service 'reach'. For example, the Department of Culture, Media and Sport (England) offers public library targets that include:

- proportion of households living within specified distance of a static library
- aggregated scheduled opening hours per 1000 population for all libraries
- number of library visits per 1000 population
- annual items added through purchase per 1000 population.

We leave you to judge how useful these targets are.

8

Thinking about evidence

> If you are working systematically through this section of the book, you have already done much of the main thinking that you need for evidence gathering. Assuming that you have thought clearly about what you are trying to achieve, how you can tell that changes are happening and what will tell you that the changes have happened, you are more than half way to cracking the problem of gathering evidence. You now need to decide how much evidence to gather.

8.1 Deciding your approach to gathering evidence

When people are faced with the prospect of gathering evidence the first reaction is often to panic. How can busy practitioners do the work of professional researchers as well? The answer is that you don't have to. Effective impact evaluation involves careful focus on what is important and then gathering the minimum amount of evidence needed to tell you what you need to know. It should be reassuring to recognize that evidence is not a separate category of information; it is information chosen by someone and gathered for a particular purpose.

8.2 The organizational context

The same evidence-collection activities may work in one place and fail somewhere else. When choosing how to gather your evidence, you need to take account of the culture of your organization, current work pressures and how ready your staff are to get involved in this work. Some of the factors to consider are:

- Other current or imminent evidence-gathering elsewhere in the organization that may compete or conflict with your efforts. (For example, when a university library decides to conduct a survey of part-time and off-campus students it knows that services to these users are a big issue for the university. It suddenly becomes a bigger issue. The governors call for a survey and the central audit team jump straight in with a hurried and poorly designed effort. This produces little of worth, but the library team has to wait for several months for the dust to settle before doing its own survey.)
- Timing: what are the best and worst times of day, week, month or year to engage with your target respondents?

- Whether your target respondents favour or dislike particular evidence-gathering methods. Have they been over-exposed to any particular methods (e.g. are they 'allergic' to questionnaires)?
- Whether the larger organization of which your service is part is averse to any method (e.g. is it disillusioned with focus groups)? This could affect the reception to any report you produce on your work.
- What methods are easiest for you and your staff to handle (including analysis of the information collected)?

8.3   Finding strong surrogates for impact evidence

When we talk about impact we are usually thinking about the impacts of services on people (service users; providers; others). As we said earlier (in Chapter 6), this entails looking for surrogates for impact because the actual impacts cannot normally be captured directly. We can classify these surrogates for impact by how strongly they convey or reflect the real impact. For example, if we interview someone immediately after they have been greatly moved by reading a particular book, this will provide a strong surrogate for impact, if the respondent can find the words to describe the experience. Sending the same person a questionnaire about their reading preferences some time later and asking the right question may result in that experience being recalled and described, but this is unlikely to have the same immediacy.

The information collected may provide a good surrogate for impact if it is detailed, specific and accurate. On the other hand, the best evidence you are able to gather may be rather generalized and approximate, that is, a weak surrogate for impact. What do you do if some of your evidence is weak? The answer is to combine it with other stronger evidence so that, overall, you are getting a good impact picture.

8.4   Matching the evidence to your needs

Now you will need to think again about why you are gathering evidence and how much to gather.

8.4.1   Why *are* you gathering evidence?

The usual reasons for collecting evidence of impact are to assure yourself that your work is making a difference or to check on how you are doing compared with other similar services. You are probably doing this to help in your own managerial role, but you may also need to convince other people inside and outside the service that it is making a difference.

If you are trying to convince other people you will have to take account of what they regard as convincing evidence even if your own views are different. Qualitative information is likely to be useful to you in gauging impact but you may have to supplement this evidence with less useful quantitative data (usually process data) if this is what the people who oversee your service expect to get. You will then have an education job – to persuade people why your evidence is more useful.

We are not saying that qualitative information is always better than quantitative information – only that it sometimes serves different purposes. Sophisticated quantitative data and good quality impact information should complement each other strongly.

Example 8.1 Combining qualitative and quantitative information

When unpacking their objective of 'Supporting the curriculum by providing materials that students can use to widen/enrich learning' a team of school librarians identified three questions that they had to answer to judge impact, as well as various ways of finding these out:

1   Is the material relevant?   *Evaluation forms*
                                            Critical incident interviews with students
                                            Talk to local education officers/advisers

2   What is the optimum level of   *Statistical performance indicators*
    use/take up?

3   How is the material used to enrich   *Asking headteachers, teachers, students*
    learning?

Both quantitative and qualitative information are needed here, to enable careful selection of material and to gauge impact, but also to show the scale of the service and whether the effort involved is proportional to the level of take-up.

8.4.2   But how much evidence *should* you gather?

The pragmatic answer to this question is 'as little as you need to make good decisions'. Evaluating impact in libraries is about making sensible decisions. Since there is no finite limit to how much evidence it is possible to acquire, there is a real danger that you can spend so much time and energy on evaluating the impact of your service that the service itself will suffer. You have to strike a balance between what you need to know, how well your evidence is telling you this, and how much of your resources you can afford to commit to this work.

Since all library-service managers are potentially 'over-tasked', with a long list of things that they must, should, could or would like to do, our own view is that impact evaluation work should concentrate on areas where you are trying to really make a difference. Traditional efficiency monitoring using process and output indicators will suffice for other areas of the service. We put this argument forward because most library-service managers have to devote much of their time, energy and effort to maintaining the service infrastructure (e.g. ensuring that service points are open and running smoothly; obtaining and deploying resources efficiently). If this is your situation, any time squeezed out for development activity is precious (and relatively expensive). It follows that much of the impact focus should be on the development work – is it having the sorts of effect that you want? Will it work better if you do some things differently? Can you use this key time better in other areas?

Ideally, as development areas demonstrate their worth they will be absorbed into the infrastructure, and efficiency monitoring is all that will be needed. This leaves you scope to concentrate on the next development area – and its impact.

8.4.3   How much evidence: different purposes

How much evidence you need to gather also depends on why you are collecting it. Standards of evidence will vary for different purposes:

- If you are gathering information mainly *to inform your own management decision-making* and future planning, we recommend that you apply the resonance test. This involves gathering a sufficient range of evidence to assure yourself that you are on the right lines. More particularly, when you present this evidence to your colleagues they agree that it sounds OK – it resonates with them. (If not, you need more evidence.)
- We apply this test when doing national research in library settings, by inviting service managers to look at what we are finding and seeing whether the picture that emerges feels right to them – if not, we gather more information in areas of doubt to the level that we feel should convince a reasonable reviewer.
- If your prime aim is to *account to the people who have an overview of your service* (e.g. senior organizational managers or local government representatives), stronger evidence will be needed, at the 'enough to convince a reasonable reviewer' level. We have already suggested that you may also need to offer more familiar evidence of efficiency as well.
- If you are making a case for *securing funds*, stronger evidence may be needed again, if you are competing with other agencies or services. Your evidence gathering will have to be at least as convincing as theirs, even before you report on the effectiveness of your service as shown through that process.
- If you receive *external funding for a project*, you will have to meet the accountability requirements of the funding organization. In our experience, these requirements can vary hugely, so it is sensible to check carefully to see what is actually required by way of evidence.

Example 8.2 Types of evidence

A helpful touchstone may be to envisage situations in which you need to convince others:

- the chief executive of your company questions whether you are providing useful information to support senior managers in their work. What evidence can you offer?

- You are talking to a senior education official about the public library role in supporting literacy or promoting reading. Will the sorts of information you assemble convince someone in that position about the difference you are making?
- The University Teaching and Learning Committee wants to strengthen the learning support provided to students. Can you make a convincing case for doing more through the library?

In each case you need to ask what such people usually rely on as evidence.

8.4.4 How reliable is your evidence?

The quantity and types of evidence are not the only issues. You also need to think about the reliability of the evidence that you are collecting. Three criteria for judging evidence (based on Thomas, 2004) are:

- **Relevance**. Does the evidence constitute information for (or against) a proposition? In impact evaluation terms, does it tell you whether or not the chosen success criteria are being met, or is it actually evidence of something else?
- **Sufficiency**. Is there corroboration with other instances of the same kind of evidence, or other kinds of evidence? In other words, is the picture consistent or are you making too much of one-off instances?
- **Veracity**. Is the process of gathering evidence free from distortion and as far as possible uncontaminated by vested interest?

We are not seeking to transform you into an academic researcher with a strong philosophical bias at this point! Instead, we suggest that you use these three criteria as a checklist when you have decided what evidence-gathering methods to use and again when you look over the evidence that you have gathered.

8.4.5 Use other people's evidence

Finally, it is worth remembering that you don't always have to generate your own evidence in order to argue a case or to take management decisions. We have reviewed the main research evidence of the established impact of different types of libraries in Chapter 3. Think about how to use this evidence to support your development work or to argue a funding case.

LAWS OF IMPACT EVALUATION 6

Be political if you are gathering information to convince other people. Give them what they want – until you have persuaded them that your evidence is more useful than what they are used to.

> **LAWS OF IMPACT EVALUATION 7**
> The case for impact evaluation is strongest in areas of service development, where time and resources are limited but real change can be demonstrated.

8.5   What counts as impact evidence?

What does evidence of impact look like and how does it manifest itself? When you focus on the impact of services on people, you are looking for changes in their attitudes or behaviour that can be attributed to these services. This takes us directly into the world of social science research. For practical purposes, you will often be combining 'traditional' efficiency measurement data with impact evidence gathered using the social science repertoire.

Borrowing from the social scientists, most of the evidence you can gather is collected in one of four ways:

* **Observe** – through structured observation, informal observation, self-recording or other means.
* **Ask people questions** – through questionnaires, interviews, focus groups etc.
* **Infer that relevant change is happening**. Two commonly used methods are to:

  — examine documents or other products created by your target groups to see if what your service is doing makes any difference. (The trick here is to look for changes that can be fairly directly linked to what your service offers. For example, if you offer students an introduction to systematic searching for information you could look for general changes in the quality of student assignments. However, more direct evidence of progress can be found by looking at the quality of bibliographies or seeing whether a wider range of sources is cited)
  — monitor the activities of the target groups using output indicators (e.g. participation in events, levels of service use, examination results). The drawback with using this traditional method is that you may find it difficult to show that these changes are influenced by what the service is doing.

* **Engage in action research**. Use these three methods of evidence-collection but as part of a systematic cyclical process. This process involves gathering evidence of impact, then collective interpretation of this evidence, leading to service modification, then back round to evidence-gathering and so on until no significant improvements are found.

8.6   Fitness for the purpose

Before we go into the variations on observation, asking questions and inferring change from the products of people's activities that form the core of the next chapter, it may be useful to think about the relationship between success criteria (and the impact indicators that explore them) and the different options for gathering evidence. It is not as simple as saying, 'If you want to find out about changes in people's attitudes – interview them', or 'Observation is the best way of noting changes in behaviour', but there is a relationship between what you are looking for and how to find it. We can take our four areas of change (affective, behavioural, knowledge-based and competence-based) as a starting point.

Affective changes

(attitudes, perceptions, levels of confidence, satisfaction with the service)
You may be able to *observe* changes in people's attitudes, but getting evidence usually involves asking the people who may or may not have changed. In particular, *asking questions* through short and tightly focused questionnaires should work, because they are neutral, but at the same time you are showing interest by asking the questions. If you are looking for evidence about people's confidence (e.g. when using ICT), questionnaires administered before and after your service intervention give people the chance to register changes without any pejorative overtones.

This is the area in which there is most potential choice when focusing on impact because we know that libraries can contribute positively to the quality of life of users in a variety of ways. (See Chapter 3.)

Example 8.3 The education library role in 'life-enhancement'

Objectives: To encourage positive student relationships with library staff and to provide a positive learning environment

Method: A well-focused user questionnaire to gather information on:

- the quality of student communication with library staff (e.g. freedom to ask questions; get support in seeking information)
- the quality of ongoing student relationships with specific library staff
- the extent to which the library provides a positive study environment (e.g. appearance and comfort; noise level etc.)
- the extent to which the library provides more direct support for study/homework (e.g. whether material can be obtained when needed; whether there are adequate photocopy facilities etc.).

Behavioural changes

(people do things differently)
Here, *observation* comes into its own, but you can also *infer changes* by looking at people's work. For example, to see change after an information-seeking input to an education

assignment, you can look at completed assignments to see the number and range of sources cited, how the sources are presented and used and how the work compares with previous assignments. If a business library seeks to increase active use by middle managers, any change in physical use can be observed, but it should also be possible to track changes by analysing enquiries and requests for documents.

Knowledge-based changes

To find out if people have learnt anything, you have to *ask them questions*. This questioning can take many forms including tests, questionnaires or focus groups. Other options are suggested in the next section. Take care not to become over-reliant on post-event questionnaires by participants. These are sometimes called 'reactionnaires', because they only really gauge whether people are positive about the experience. As Burrows and Berardinelli (2003) note:

> While learner interest and motivation are certainly factors in the outcomes
> of training, there is not a direct relationship between the learner's perception
> of training and actual learning, especially at the time when the learner has
> just completed the training experience.

If you really want to find out whether your training interventions have made a difference it is probably best to contact some of the participants a few months later and ask.

Competence-based changes

(people do things more effectively)

How can you tell whether people are more competent? You can *ask them questions*, but also ask other people who *observe* them doing things. When asking people to assess their own change you can use the same range of methods as for knowledge-based questioning (including the additional options listed below). To pick up on what other people see, it depends who the people are and whether they are willing to give you feedback. Potential respondents may be work colleagues of the people you are interested in, other students or teachers. Interviews are usually the most viable method for evidence-gathering of this sort, because informants may feel uncomfortable about making judgements on other people in writing.

An alternative way to throw light on the level and variety of user skills (or of skills weaknesses) is to analyse a sample of enquiries recorded by your service. Service records are typically used to review the demands on the service, but they can also be used to tell you about what your users are struggling with. An analysis schedule could be constructed for this purpose.

The comments made about training under the previous heading also apply to learning new skills.

Other methods of gathering impact evidence

In a recent impact-evaluation programme, ten teams of UK university library staff used the following methods to gather impact evidence in relation to e-information services and e-learning innovations (Markless and Streatfield, 2006):

- Where the focus is on the *impact of services on students:*

  — tests (including online diagnostic tests)
  — questionnaires and embedded questions
  — focus groups
  — interviews conducted while students were conducting searches
  — student diaries
  — progress files
  — student bibliography analysis (adopted in five universities).

- Where the focus is on *academic staff* the choice of methods depends on the purpose:

  — to gather staff perceptions about service impact: structured face-to-face or telephone interview (four universities)
  — for more specific baseline evidence: focus groups
  — to evaluate co-operation or collaboration between academic and library staff: records of contacts between these groups
  — for evidence of change in academic staff: analyse their lists of recommended reading and e-links for students.

  (One team also undertook an information literacy teaching audit covering the whole university.)

- Where *specific information literacy inputs* are made by library staff:

  — monitoring of information literacy outcomes or of assignments that require students to deploy a research strategy
  — observation of student engagement by other library staff.

A useful observation for busy library-service managers was that interviews produce 'fairly instant results' – that is, the evidence can be used almost immediately to improve service delivery.

Finally, we want to re-emphasize how important it is to be clear about the nature of the changes you are trying to achieve (success criteria and impact indicators). This gives you powerful clues about how to collect your evidence.

9

Gathering and interpreting evidence

This chapter suggests which evidence gathering methods will tell you what you need to know, how to gather that evidence, and what that evidence is telling you. We then offer a warning about confusing evidence with advocacy.

Let us start with a precept: all evidence-gathering methods have inherent weaknesses, so it is important to employ a range of methods if you want to build up a good picture – this is known in the research jargon as triangulation.

Since it is probably better to adapt a research tool (such as a questionnaire, checklist or observation schedule) for your own purposes rather than start from scratch, we have prepared or selected a range of research tools for use in different types of libraries. These tools can be found at www.facetpublishing.co.uk/evaluatingimpact.

Even if you are adapting an existing research tool there are a number of things that you should bear in mind when using them to gather evidence. These are considered below.

9.1 Observation

At first sight, it is surprising that library and information research borrows heavily on two of the social science research approaches (asking questions and making inferences) but largely neglects systematic observation as a research method. It is easy to understand this under-use in large-scale research, since systematic observation is time-consuming and can generate huge amounts of data. However, even when people take on small-scale evaluation they usually gravitate towards the questionnaire and the focus group, almost regardless of whether these will provide the sorts of information required.

This is a pity, because in the immortal words of the American baseball player and coach Lawrence 'Yogi' Berra, 'You can observe a lot by watching.' We know from our own experience that observation is a great way to develop ideas about how people use information, how library systems and services can be improved or how people can improve their teaching, training or interaction with service users. It is also one of the best ways of finding out whether your services are really making an impact.

There are at least four types of observation that may prove useful in evaluating the impact of your services.

9.1.1   Small-scale systematic observation

If you are interested in specific aspects of service use, such as how users find things in your library, or what they actually use your computers or wireless links for, a time-series study may be the answer. This involves gathering small amounts of information at predetermined times, spread over different times of day, week, term or year (depending on how much variation you think is likely). The advantage of this approach is that it only involves a member of your staff remembering (and if necessary being prompted) to collect and record a small amount of information at any one time. This recording can be done by making notes of what is happening from any convenient viewing point, or doing a tour of the relevant part of the library to see, for example, what is showing on computer screens. These records will soon build up into a fairly detailed picture of use, which may differ interestingly from what you predict. There are of course ethical issues involved here, and your organization may have a code of ethics or a research ethics committee that will have to be taken into account. In any case, individuals should not be identified in your observation records without their permission.

A variation on this theme is to record interesting events as they happen. For example, if a particular group of potential users makes little use of your service, and becomes the target for service development, any instance of use by members of that group is relevant evidence.

Although large-scale observation will be too expensive to be feasible, focused and systematic observation of student activity in the library is certainly possible. You could consider watching students doing a library-based assignment; more general observation at prescribed intervals would be useful too. To get real evidence in this way you will need to use an observation schedule designed, for example, to assess the information skills of students. (See sections 9.9 and 9.10 for access to a range of tools to help.)

9.1.2   Informal observation

Front-line library staff and their managers spend a large part of their time in observing what is going on, but there is usually little incentive to note what is happening, even if there is time to do so. All this changes when you focus on particular areas of service impact. Suddenly all observations about that part of the service are 'grist to the mill'. All that is needed is to alert colleagues to the fact that these aspects of service are now being looked at and to invite them to record anything that they see that they feel may be of interest as evidence (ideally for an agreed and limited time period). For this to work, you need to share with them what you are interested in finding out more about and why, so that they are in the picture and can include you in the part of the picture that they see.

9.1.3   Peer observation

This approach is much favoured in educational settings as a way of giving immediately relevant feedback to teachers in the classroom. You can adopt a broadly similar approach in looking at interaction with library users, as a way of stimulating reflection and improving professional practice. At a minimum all that is needed is two willing participants and sufficient time to allow one to observe the other in action and give feedback afterwards. The participants will need to agree on what aspects of the interaction they will look at, will probably need to secure permission from service users immediately affected by the observation, and some should have some ground rules for feedback (such as 'positive comments first').

If you work in higher education and your institution has a formal teaching-staff appraisal programme, you may like to follow the example of one college that we have worked with and adapt it to include encounters between students and library staff at the enquiry desk. Peer observation is now accepted practice in higher education and most universities have criteria in place to support the process. Find out who is managing academic peer review in your institution and see what they can provide to help you.

9.1.4   Accompanied visits

This activity is regularly used by museums education staff who want to find out how people are really responding to their exhibitions. If you conduct an exit interview and ask people whether they felt lost at all when going round the exhibition, nobody ever admits to it. But if you accompany people round an exhibition, observe what they do and ask a few discreet questions, you will find that most people are confused about where they are and where the exhibition is leading them most of the time! Transferred to a library context the accompanied visit can provide a valuable picture of the interaction between the user (especially the new user) and the institution. Accompanying new users of the service on their first visit may throw some light on the phenomenon identified by former UK Education Inspector Trevor Dickenson who described the library experience as 'intimidation by furniture'.

9.1.5   Taking pictures

Although this is not a separate category of observation, there may be times when taking still or moving pictures of an event or activity will add a lot to the evidence of the impact of what you are doing. Remember not to do this with children without getting written permission from parents or guardians in advance.

9.1.6   Observation for other reasons – work shadowing

Since we are observation enthusiasts, we hope that we will be forgiven for adding that observation is not just useful in collecting evidence of impact. One particular form of mutual observation, *work shadowing*, can be used to focus on or raise questions about aspects of library processes and procedures that staff have come to take for granted. This can be done by 'parachuting in' library-service managers from elsewhere, to look at what you do and give you feedback in agreed areas (before you do the same for them).

Work shadowing is useful in any library setting where users have particular ways of working that library staff need to know about. Arranging work shadowing with managers, professional staff (such as the legal professions), researchers or teachers should help library staff to work more closely with them and to understand their information worlds and priorities. Better yet, this type of reciprocal observation exchange frequently leads to closer co-operation between the people involved around projects and work programmes.

A variation on this approach is to change work roles. A UK public library service recently introduced a 'Back to front' programme, in which senior managers spent time in front-line library roles (and vice versa). When the county librarian spends a day at a branch library enquiry point, she finds that staff spend more time looking at the computer screen than interacting with enquirers. As a direct result she makes sure that the new computer screens being purchased can readily be swivelled so that the enquirer can see what is being found. All the staff in this programme (including managers from the chief executive's office and other parts of the local authority) have to write an evaluation report focused on the part of the service that they have looked at.

Work shadowing may also give rise to ideas for improving your services so that they have even more impact.

9.2   Asking questions

'Asking questions' encompasses the ubiquitous questionnaire survey, individual or group interviews, focus groups and such hybrid activities as getting interview respondents to look at a website and relay their thoughts and feelings to the interviewer via the telephone or face-to-face.

9.2.1   Questionnaire surveys

We have put these first because this is the method that library-service managers tend to go for if they start to think about impact – unfortunately!

Public library services have traditionally relied heavily on service-performance (usually output) statistics, such as enrolments and loans, backed by the occasional questionnaire survey. We have viewed hundreds of library-service questionnaires and this may be the time to offer some comments:

- Many questions are too general and too bland to do more than show that libraries are well regarded by users.
- Others overreach themselves by trying to gather complex information that is more appropriate for interviews.

- Many are poorly designed – with embedded library jargon, sloppy wording and little variety of task.
- Very few are adequately pilot-tested to iron out problems before they are used.
- Most show evidence that they were produced in too much of a hurry. Constructing and testing a properly designed questionnaire from scratch takes at least one person-week.

Overall, too many questionnaires unwittingly project the designers' preconceptions out to potential respondents and have them reflected back by nice people who are trying to second guess what the designers mean. Questionnaires are a good method of gathering small amounts of specific information through structured sequences of questions – when you already have an idea of what range of replies is likely and have a feel for the language which the people you are surveying use to discuss the concepts that interest you.

What about sample sizes and response rates?

There are no hard and fast rules about the proportion of your total target audience that you need to involve in your survey, although a higher proportion will make it less likely that you will pick up a totally unrepresentative group of respondents. If you want to get an informative response to questions about the impact of specific interventions or parts of the service, 10% of the target group should give you a good picture, if these are selected randomly. (You may want to ensure that your sample is 'stratified' to ensure that you include particular groups within your target audience, for example, a business library may want to ensure that all the main levels of management are included.)

If you are thinking about bigger-scale surveys and you want to gather statistically significant data (e.g. if you are trying to predict likely future demand for services) – you need to get professional advice from people who are expert in conducting surveys.

The most important thing to say about the response rate to a questionnaire survey is that if you get less than 50% of completed questionnaires returned you know nothing at all about the views of more than half of the people that you asked. Making decisions on the basis of a low response rate is another form of guesswork.

9.2.2 Towards better questionnaires

Below are some ground rules for designing effective questionnaires.

Give attention to the structure of the questionnaire

- Start with a straightforward question to get the recipient to begin replying.
- Try to ensure some variety in the types of question asked (see below).

- Draw skidpaths if there are alternative routes (of the type 'if 'Yes' go on to question x', with a line showing the route) to make sure that every eventuality is covered. Then choose whether to leave these lines in to help people move through the questionnaire.
- Group related topics into modules.
- Move from the general to the specific in each section (usually).
- Make the structure clear to the respondent by using headings.

Choose the question types to fit the purpose

The main options are:

- **closed questions**. These can be 'yes' and 'no' boxes or a wider range of categories that you offer people to choose from. Make sure that each category is distinct and that all eventualities are covered. If you are completing a questionnaire and find that your preferred response category is not provided, what does this say about the competence of the designers? A useful catch all category is 'Anything else? Please say what', but only if you leave enough space for people to add their own categories.

  — Closed questions are becoming more common with the increased use of electronic questionnaires linked to analysis tools that can aggregate replies almost instantly. Unfortunately, the ease of access to such tools can lead to closed questions being set when open questions are more appropriate.
  — A common type of closed question involves time periods (e.g. at least weekly, at least monthly, less than once a month) or age ranges (e.g. 1–20, 21–30 etc.). It may sound silly, but a common fault with this type of question is to offer overlapping categories (e.g. up to 20, 20 to 40).

- **open questions**. At its simplest this may be a 'Why is this?' after a closed question. However you phrase the question, it must be unambiguous – your aim is for the respondents to understand it and to reply in their own words.

  — Don't forget that you will have to analyse all the replies to open questions and that categorization of the replies and then synthesis take time.
  — There are several research data analysis tools available to help process qualitative information. Even so, there is no substitute for engaging with the 'raw' replies to ensure that you understand what the evidence is telling you.

Example 9.1 The hazards in setting closed questions

This example is from an electronic student self-assessment tool:

Using search engines

If your search gives you too many hits do you:

   ❏ Look at the first few items?
   ❏ Narrow your search by adding additional search terms?
   ❏ Try a different search engine?
   ❏ Give up searching?

This question almost slipped through, although it did not include one of the best ways to proceed: review the search terms and modify them to increase precision.

Use checklists or response scales where appropriate

These are a form of closed question. Most common are:

- **Simple checklists**, for example:

  What was the **main thing** you were doing in the library today?

Working on a course project or assignment	❏
Reading related to my course	❏
Other reading	❏
Exam revision	❏
Looking for specific information in the library	❏
Using the internet for coursework	❏
Using the internet for personal interest	❏
Photocopying	❏
Just visiting	❏
Other: please say what!	❏

  Please tick one box only

- **Likert scales**: a set of choices to record strength of agreement/disagreement, for example:

  By 2010 sophisticated subject-focused search engines will be the normal method of gaining access to internet resources.

Highly likely	❏	❏	❏	❏	❏	❏ **Highly unlikely**
Highly desirable	❏	❏	❏	❏	❏	❏ **Highly undesirable**

  Please tick one box only

- **Thurlstone scales**: forced choice to agree/disagree, for example:

  Are you confident when using **health websites?**   ❏ Yes   No ❏

- **Semantic differential**: seeking quantitative measures in areas that are usually addressed through qualitative means, by offering scales between extremes, for example:

  The Company Information Service is:

Good	❑	❑	❑	❑	❑	❑	Bad
Unfriendly	❑	❑	❑	❑	❑	❑	Friendly
Active	❑	❑	❑	❑	❑	❑	Passive
Relevant	❑	❑	❑	❑	❑	❑	Irrelevant
Slow	❑	❑	❑	❑	❑	❑	Rapid
Reliable	❑	❑	❑	❑	❑	❑	Unreliable

  Please tick one box only in each row

  These scales have to be carefully constructed to be effective. It is probably better to use ready-made versions than to invent your own.

- **Guttman scales**: statements arranged in sequence to gauge the strength of the respondent's view, for example:

  Within your subject discipline:

  Electronic journals will completely replace paper-based journals
  within ten years   ❑
  Electronic journals will gradually replace paper-based journals   ❑
  There will continue to be a place for paper-based journals
  alongside e-journals   ❑
  Paper-based journals will be preferred to e-journals for the
  foreseeable future   ❑
  There will be a reaction against e-journals in favour of
  paper-based journals   ❑

  Please tick the box that most accurately reflects your own view.

Instructions and wording

It is important to heed the following advice:

- Offer clear and consistent instructions for completing the questionnaire (this is easily forgotten if questions are considered individually). For closed questions, do you want people to choose one box (e.g. the most important category for their work) or all relevant boxes?

- Pay attention to question wording (avoid ambiguities; negative statements in the question; jargon, except that of the respondents; and enmeshing two or more questions together).

To summarize, the overall aim of the evaluation questionnaire is to obtain relevant information efficiently. You need active co-operation from your target group when doing this. Anything that will help people to co-operate with you by carefully completing and returning your questionnaire should be actively encouraged. This takes time, planning and attention to detail – even before you reach the data-analysis stage.

LAWS OF IMPACT EVALUATION 8
Questionnaire surveys are ideal for projecting the compiler's preconceptions and prejudices and having them confirmed by an invisible audience. They are also quite useful for collecting small amounts of information from a sample of respondents or all respondents within a target group.

9.3   Interviewing

According to Michael Brenner (Brenner, Brown and Canter, 1985) 'the research interview is an artificial conversation designed to collect research-relevant data.' The element of artifice is provided by the fact that one person is answering all the questions and the other one is asking these questions and recording all the answers. As to data collection, it follows that anything (within reason) that helps to achieve this end is desirable and that all other behaviour is not. As we show below, respondents sometimes have to be taught their role as respondents, especially if they are inclined to be flippant or to wander from the question.

There are four main types of research interview:

- In the **structured interview**, all questions are asked in a predetermined order from a prepared schedule and each time a question is asked this should be done in the same way and with the same emphasis. This type of interview is probably the norm in library-service evaluation.
- In the **exploratory interview**, the question areas are predetermined but the respondents are allowed some latitude to answer in their own way. The interviewer may probe for more information in promising areas. The exploratory interview is particularly valuable at the early stages of evidence-gathering to identify issues and find out what concepts and terminology various groups of people use. (For example, 'information literacy' is a good word to use with education librarians but not with lecturers – in the UK they prefer 'study skills', 'library skills' or even 'problem-solving skills' – elsewhere you can find out the preferred terms by doing exploratory interviews.)
- A **semi-structured interview** is a one-sided conversation in which the respondent is allowed free rein as long as the interviewer considers that what is being said is, or might be, relevant. This works well with experts, who usually have a strong

theoretical basis to their thinking that will be explicated by letting them talk. The 'Catch 22' here is that although reliability is likely to be improved by increased structure, too much structure may inhibit responses or produce little of consequence.

- **Passive interviewing** is important in library-service evaluation but isn't usually recognized as interviewing at all. Most library staff who are involved with users, and many who aren't, receive lots of passing comments about aspects of the service. In some libraries, staff are encouraged to note down relevant comments and these may be fed into reports. For the most part, such comments are not recorded because there is no reason to do so. As we have suggested with informal observation above, all this changes when you focus on particular areas of service impact. Once there is a focus, all comments about that part of the service are potentially useful. You will need to alert colleagues to the fact that comments on this aspect of service are now relevant (again for an agreed and limited time period), introduce a mechanism for recording the comments (such as a set of forms at each service point) and, ideally, provide an incentive to your staff to keep these records!

9.3.1   Designing an interview schedule

If you are going to use structured or semi-structured interviews, first you will have to choose or design your interview schedule. Here are some of the ground rules for interview-schedule design. Most of them also apply to planning your question areas for semi-structured interviews:

- Ease the respondent into the interview. For example, you can start with a question about their work responsibilities to get them talking comfortably, assuming that this information is relevant. Don't ask for personal information early in an interview.
- Adopt a logical structure by grouping questions into sections and proceeding from the general to the specific.
- Share this structure with the respondents so that they know where the conversation is going. Offer a brief introductory outline of the areas to be covered; this can be reinforced as each new section is reached (e.g. 'Now I'm going to ask you some questions about how you use information at work').
- Vary the bill of fare. You can combine closed questions (such as 'Do you ever go to the company information centre?') and open questions (e.g. 'What kinds of use do you make of that service?'). You can vary the respondents' task further by, for instance, asking them to select replies and tick boxes on response cards or to choose one of a set of descriptive vignettes that matches their own information-related behaviour; or again you may want to show people an information publication and ask them for comments.
- Make sure that the questions are clear and in spoken English, rather than the more formal written version, which sounds stilted when it is read. (Which form is being used here?) Try to avoid using negatives in questions (they can be confusing); and choose any jargon deliberately to reflect respondents' usage. Library and information

jargon should be avoided (asking lecturers about serials has been known to elicit strange responses!).

Test out the schedule in pilot interviews. Try to avoid:

- questions that are difficult to ask (too many questions in one, sentences that are too long, tongue-twisters)
- questions that are difficult to answer (e.g. that contain unfamiliar words or phrases, that ask for generalizations or abstractions, hypothetical questions; don't ask busy operational staff about how they divide up their time – they probably don't)
- questions that invite distortion (leading questions that carry assumptions that the people interviewed may not share; don't ask respondents about the opinions or behaviour of other people).

Most of the principles outlined here also apply to questionnaire design.

9.3.2 Setting up and administering the interview

Let us assume that your 'victim' has agreed to be interviewed. What next?

- Choose a neutral venue if possible (a meeting room or spare office is ideal). If you have to use your respondent's office, avoid the 'client chair' on the other side of the desk: if necessary move it to one end of the desk so that you are not in the usual 'grilling position'.
- Check that the interview is still convenient (this is especially important for telephone interviews – anything may be happening at the other end!). If there is a problem, reschedule the interview. You want a respondent who is concentrating on your interview.
- Ask if any telephone calls can be diverted to save time (if you think this will work).
- Make sure that the respondent knows who you are and what you are trying to find out in general terms (an introductory letter is usual but a reminder may still be needed).
- Explain that the respondent can refuse to answer any question if they wish.
- Explain whether the interview is confidential: a common phrase is 'We will not be reporting anything in a form that could lead to your replies being identifiable.' If a respondent later baulks at a question, it may be enough to remind them that the interview is confidential to get a reply.
- If you wish to record (on tape or electronically), ask permission and say how you will use the recording. Position the recorder where your respondent can reach it and show them how to turn it off if they want to say anything off the record.

If you have organized and conducted the interview well, it is very rare for people to curtail the process. Only a few respondents will cavil at particular questions and only one or two interviews turn out to be useless.

9.3.3   Doing the interview

Once you have chosen the type of interview, you can do a lot to create good interview conditions, 'train' the respondents to perform their task and reduce incomprehension or resistance. In the end, though, to be a good interviewer you need be effective in the five main areas of research interviewing:

- **ask the question**. Read the question at 'slow normal' speed and in a neutral tone, but with emphasis on certain words to help the respondent understand the question.
- **listen to the reply**. This is usually the easy bit because the replies should be interesting if your questions are good. Don't get distracted if the respondent sounds boring: the most monotonous replies can turn out to be full and revealing.

The other three areas: non-directive probes and prompts; recording answers; and feeding back complex replies are covered in more detail below.

Non-directive probes and prompts

Ensure that the respondent **answers in full** by using non-directive probes or prompts. The aim here is to get answers to the question without influencing the answers accidentally by putting words into people's mouths or directing them towards one kind of answer.

Non-directive probes

If you want someone to answer a question in more depth, try a **non-directive probe**, such as:

- **the silent probe**. You ask a question and get a superficial or cryptic answer. Wait, with pen poised. This is all that is usually needed to get the respondent to elaborate. Even a ten-second pause can feel like eternity if you are on the receiving end.
- **the encouragement probe** (semi-verbal). You make a noise to show that you are listening and interested – such as 'ahah' or 'erhem'. This is a concession to the one-sided nature of the conversation. It can be disconcerting if you are being interviewed and are talking away but getting no response at all. The sorts of grunts advocated here seem ludicrous when written down but work well in practice. As soon as you move away from non-verbal cues you are in danger of influencing people's answers. For example, if you say 'yes' from time to time, are you agreeing with the respondent?
- **the elaboration probe**. You can ask a respondent to explain an answer, but take care not to offer your own interpretation in case they just take the easy way out and agree to your version. Often, all you have to do to get someone to be clearer is to repeat the part of the answer that puzzles you. If that doesn't work, add 'What did you mean by that please?'

Non-directive prompts

You ask a question and the respondent doesn't answer. Try one of the following **non-directive prompts**:

- **give time** for the person to answer. Strictly speaking, this is not a prompt, but remember that your respondents are hearing your question for the first time. They may need time to think; keep silent to encourage them to do so.
- **dealing with a challenge**. If the respondent asks whether your question means A or B you have a quick decision to make. Your main options are:

  — **repetition**. If you think that the respondent hasn't fully grasped the question, you should repeat it.
  — **interpretation**. If the respondent asks which meaning is intended, try saying 'Whatever it means to you'. This usually works (but make a note of the problem – you may have to revise the question later).
  — **neutral adjudication**. If the respondent is still struggling, reword the question (and make a note of your exact words so that you can review the question and answer afterwards, and if necessary discard both).

- **predetermined prompts**. Pilot the interview questions properly in advance to make sure you are aware of potential hazards. You are then in a position to prepare definitions or clarifications in advance and give them when asked.
- **challenge prompts**. People aren't always consistent in their replies during an interview. If you think that a reply is inconsistent with something said earlier, refer back to the previous answer and remind the respondent what he or she said. This is usually enough to get an explanation.

Record the answers

The huge beginner's mistake is to forget to do this (we have large amounts of videotape evidence to prove it!). You should take notes even if you are recording the interview as this will help you to make sense of the replies at the time and give you a quick route into the interview. Remember that it takes about five hours to transcribe fully one hour of a recording. If you are not recording by other means, try to capture as much as possible of what people say in their own words. This should be the hard job. If you are finding it easy you are probably not probing enough – so why bother interviewing?

Feed back complex replies

You should do this to make sure that you have understood them and to prompt further comment. This takes confidence but is well worth doing.

All of these areas can cause difficulties, but most people can get to perform better in each one through focused training and reflection on their own performance.

Points to watch while interviewing

- **Body language**. You can convey alertness as well as interest in what is being said (or the opposite!) through your posture. More specifically, you can show that you are listening by establishing eye contact. To signal that you have 'switched off' (if someone is talking too much or wandering from the point) simultaneously look down and stop writing.
- **Pace**. You can control your own speed of speech as well as the length of the pause after your respondent has finished a sentence before you ask the next question. Aim for a relaxed, deliberate and thoughtful tone to the encounter.
- **Neutrality**. Do not show agreement, disagreement, approval or disapproval at anything the respondent says. Over-concern with establishing a friendly relationship can reduce an interview to a sociable chat.

9.3.4   The critical incident interview

This special form of structured interview is most useful to find out about interactions between library-service users and the services used. It is especially useful as a way to evaluate enquiry services. The standard approach is to select 20 to 50 substantial enquiries (not requests for contact addresses etc.) which form the critical incidents. Then:

1 Arrange telephone interviews with the enquirers.
2 At the beginning of the interview, remind the enquirer about the particular contact with your service (using the enquiry record completed at the time). Two difficulties here are:

- The enquirer may only have hazy recall of the particular incident (options: proceed and hope that memory returns or negotiate discussion of a more recent and memorable enquiry).
- The enquirer may not think of the chosen enquiry as an enquiry at all! They may think that it was a conversational gambit or part of an information exchange with library staff (if this is the case, proceed but record the different interpretation of what was going on).

3 Glean contextual information. Ask the enquirers why they were seeking that information at that time (what triggered them to make the contact, what was happening in their organization or in their own life that brought this to the fore). Also ask what other information sources were tried and why.
4 Evaluation: what useful information, if any, did the enquirer get from any of the sources tried and why was it useful? (And if relevant, how did your response compare with other people's?)
5 Quality assurance: how well and how politely did your staff respond? (People do tend to remember outstandingly good treatment as well as the opposite.)

6 Impact: did the enquirer use the information provided by your service and, if so, did anything happen as a result?

7 General comments on the enquirer's experience of your services.

This way of looking at enquiries tends to give a better picture of how the service fits into the evolving world of a range of users, as well as of the main factors that lead people to make enquiries. The approach also provides a way for enquirers to make direct comparisons of services (including such elements as format and presentation). It can produce occasional but powerful information about the real impact of information on people's life and work, because it offers a very specific and direct focus for the user to make a judgement.

More strategically, you can readily translate sets of interviews into case studies as evidence. Perhaps most importantly, service managers report that they find this type of information useful in evaluating and then fine tuning their services in ways that traditional evaluation approaches don't touch.

9.3.5   Conducting a semi-structured interview

All the tactics outlined in section 9.3.3 apply equally to semi-structured interviews. In addition, you can use *directional probes* to obtain:

- **retrospective elaboration or clarification**. Refer back to earlier remarks made by the respondent but in neutral terms, such as: 'Earlier you said . . . could you tell me more about that?' (elaboration) or 'What did you do as a result?' (clarification).

This tactic should be used sparingly. Try to use the respondent's own words whenever you refer to something said earlier.

9.3.6   Telephone interviews

The individual face-to-face interview offers the most straightforward route to gathering relevant information. You can explore issues in depth and can note and analyse the fine points of people's responses. Unfortunately, the face-to-face interview is expensive of your time, especially if the likely respondents are geographically scattered.

Telephone interviews offer many, but not all, of the advantages of the face-to-face encounter and can be more efficient to organize and carry through. They can also be an effective means of garnering evidence, as long as the ground rules are observed. Most of the preparatory steps are the same as for the face-to-face interview. The following guidelines are important:

- Explain to the potential respondent what you are trying to achieve and why, preferably in the initial contact letter (or e-mail).

- Suggest how contact should be established. If you write to introduce yourself and your project, say that you will phone to find out whether the recipient is willing to be interviewed and when is a convenient time.
- Always follow up by phone within the period that you specify. The aim at this point is to allay any concerns about being interviewed and to arrange a convenient interview time. Try to offer a realistic estimate of the amount of time required for the interview (based on your pilot tests of the interview). Be ready to do the interview on the spot if that is what the respondent strongly prefers.
- When dealing with people at work, it will take two to three contact calls on average to catch up with your potential 'victim' if that person is at operational or middle-management level. In general, the more strategic the respondent, the higher the average number of contact calls required.
- Always phone when you said you would phone, reintroduce yourself (you are only one of many voices at the other end of the line) and check to see that the timing is still convenient. If it isn't, reschedule the call.
- The main irritant here is that the respondent may not be playing by the same rules! Relatively few people book telephone interviews into their diary in the same way as face-to-face interviews. They may have completely forgotten the appointment and be away from the office or even on vacation when you dutifully phone up. The good news is that if they do miss the appointment a plaintive message to say that you phoned as promised is usually enough to get better co-operation next time. Be ready for the conscience-stricken respondent who phones back as soon as they return to the office, all ready to talk.
- Try to avoid interviewing people on their mobile phone. Apart from the obvious matter of cost, this kind of contact diminishes any influence that you might have over the environment in which the respondent is trying to concentrate on (or even to hear) your questions.
- Conversely, phoning someone at their office or home should ensure a reasonable environment for the conversation and is the best possible way of reducing the effects of the 'Great Interrupter' – the telephone! (Even so, the occasional respondent will interrupt the call to field another one.)

Conducting the interview again follows the lines of the face-to-face version but with several constraints. Naturally, unless you have the latest in cellular technology, you can't see your respondent. This means that you miss all of the small clues of body language and facial expression that add texture to the interview. Similarly, the respondent can't see you. Any pause at the other end of the telephone line feels much more lengthy than it actually is, so, if you are taking detailed notes (and if not, why are you bothering at all?), tell the respondent what you are doing.

Although respondents usually appear to concentrate quite carefully during telephone interviews, a lengthy interview will feel longer. The ideal length for a telephone interview is probably about 30 minutes, whereas a 45-minute version face-to-face would probably not feel long.

The other constraints are more psychological in character. Many people do not like speaking on the telephone (and this includes some library-service managers); some seem to find it more difficult to develop a train of thought on the phone and a few have evolved such a staccato telephone manner that it may be hard to hear or interpret what is being said or to coax out much useful information.

9.4 Getting impact information from people in groups

One way to get at impact is to bring together a group of users of the service to pool their thoughts on how your services affect them. Don't let this turn into a test of who has the loudest voice or most articulate opinions.

9.4.1 Brainstorming

Two ways to pick people's brains and still retain control over the process are individual and structured brainstorming.

Individual brainstorming

Group participants round a table and invite them to think about their answers to a carefully chosen question, such as 'What are the key improvements that need to be made to the library website to ensure that people take notice of it?' Ask them to write their individual replies on sticky notes, using one sheet for each idea, and to pool the results in the middle of the table. Then invite them to cluster the sheets in whatever way they think works (there will be overlaps; get participants to stick these together), sorting out what the statements mean as they go along and labelling each cluster themselves (this will tell you how they describe the concept.) You can then focus discussion on each of these clusters in turn, using open questions such as 'What are the issues or concerns here?'

General points to remember:

* Focus the discussion on the clusters and listen carefully to each person in turn.
* Ensure that someone is recording the discussion – you are too busy!

Just because people are assembled as a group doesn't mean that you have to work with them as a group.

Structured brainstorming

To carry out structured brainstorming (such as the Nominal Group Technique outlined here), seat participants (ideally about 7–12 people) in a horseshoe formation around a table, with you and a flip-chart stand at the open end. Ask them to record their responses to your evaluation question (as for individual brainstorming above). However, this time you ask them to record their answers in short phrases on their own note pads.

Don't give way to the temptation to rush this stage. Allow a good five minutes for them to come up with ideas. When people stop writing, ask each person *in turn* to offer one item to the pooled list. Write these in their words on the flip chart, numbering each one. Keep going round until people run out of ideas (usually 30–60 ideas). Be inclusive; if in doubt, write it up on the flip-chart. Display all the sheets as you go along. Put off any discussion of the ideas until the next stage.

Sooner or later someone will buck the rules and try to launch into a long explanation of their idea. Ask that person to summarize the idea in a short phrase and say you will collect it next time around, then move on to the next person. This is a good process control mechanism to ensure that the group stays nominal (a group in name only)!

When all the ideas are in, look at each flip-chart sheet in turn and ask the group to see if they are sure what each phrase means (some ideas may be too cryptic). Stress that you *don't* want them to say if they agree or disagree with the propositions at this stage. Then the group may wish to link a few overlapping ideas. Next, invite people to choose the five most important items from the list (important for them individually, or for your service – you decide beforehand). When they have all chosen the appropriate numbers, either get them to tick their five choices on the displayed sheets, or you record their numbers in priority order (most important first – use a different coloured pen) by writing numbers 1–5 for each person on the displayed sheets. (You may then like to weight these scores from first choice = 5 points, downwards, using another different colour, and add up the total points for each idea.) You are now ready to discuss participants' high priority items.

General points to remember:

- Actively discourage discussion until *after* the prioritization stage.
- Timings: individual recording of ideas 5–10 minutes (this will feel like 5 hours the first time around, but you must give people time to think); round up of ideas c.30 minutes; ranking 5 minutes; scoring (ticking, or you writing) 5 minutes; ranking (offer a break while you do this) 5 minutes; discussion c.30 minutes.

Both the activities just described can work well as part of a focus group.

There are literally thousands of tried and tested group activities, including many that are specifically designed to collect and prioritize information. Consult a friendly trainer about what sorts of impact information you are trying to obtain. Most trainers have a good repertoire of group activities for particular purposes.

9.4.2   Card sort activities

Meanwhile, if you want to get people to try to prioritize and discuss propositions, various types of card-sort activity should give you focused information (and they are fun to do).

To stimulate discussion about general service impact or the effect of specific services on users, generate your own set of key propositions in relation to your theme; then type and stick each proposition on 5in. x 3in. cards or sticky notes (about 20–24 propositions are ideal; number them to help in de-briefing later). Divide people into *small* groups (not more than four people); then ask them to sort one set of the cards per group in response to your research question. Your question should be about the impact of the service on them as users. You can get them to do this in one of several ways, such as through a self-directed or more structured nine-diamond task:

- **Self-directed task** – ask people to organize the cards into a meaningful pattern, shape or flowchart, adding their own ideas on blank sheets if they wish. Then de-brief each group in turn by asking them to explain what they have produced and why, picking up on points of similarity and difference between groups.
- **Nine-diamond task** – ask people to reject all but nine of the cards (they can substitute their own ideas on blank cards at this point) and arrange the chosen nine in diamond formation (the words below each represent one card) in descending order of importance or priority:

FIRST

SECOND TIER

THE THIRD TIER

FOURTH TIER

FIFTH

The idea of this nine-diamond activity is to encourage people to prioritize without wasting time over the 'in-between' rank order (for example, by trying to exactly rank the three items in the third tier). De-brief across the groups by asking what people placed first and why, what went into the second tier and why; what people threw out easily and why; and what they added in (if anything) and why.

When the process is complete, the diamonds can be 'translated' into weighted scores (and the totals for each item added to represent the overall priorities across the participants) as follows:

Items on Tier 1–5 points

Items on Tier 2–4 points

Items on Tier 3–3 points

Items on Tier 4–2 points

Items on Tier 5–1 point.

You can then compare the results of different groups doing the same exercise, and thus gather information about the impact of services.

General points to remember:

- You will need one set of cards per group and a 'master' list for yourself.
- Allow ample time (25-30 minutes) for people to sort their cards (including small group discussion).
- If members of a group can't agree on priorities, ask them to remember and report back what they disagreed about at the de-briefing stage.

- If you are working with several groups, wait until the second one finishes, from there on invite the groups as they finish to look at each others' output – but keep them away from groups that are still working.
- When all the groups have finished, start the de-briefing. Allow ample time for de-briefing (a rule of thumb is 15 minutes if there are two groups, then 5 more for each additional group).
- Use a flip chart to catch most of the content and, if possible, get a colleague to take notes of the discussion.

This exercise is a good way of equipping people with the concepts that they might not otherwise have. This will enable them to discuss the chosen question in a general way.
Requirements for the nine-diamond activity:

- space for participants to work in small groups
- enough time (c. one hour) to conduct the activity
- a facilitator for the activity (following the steps set out above)
- a note taker to record the feedback from groups
- sets of slips/cards
- a flipchart and working pens.

Example 9.1 A set of nine-diamond concepts used in an education library

In this case the aim is to get students to say which of the following elements of the service make any difference to them when they are studying:

1	Books borrowed from the library
2	Reference books in the library
3	CD-ROMs in the library
4	Internet access from the library
5	Project folders
6	Magazines/journals
7	The library enquiries/help desk (use locally preferred term)
8	Library induction
9	Photocopying
10	Being shown how to use PCs to find things by a librarian
11	Sessions by a librarian on how to use the library/search for information
12	Current newspapers
13	Old newspapers
14	Videos
15	Interlibrary loans
16	The library catalogue
17	Leaflets/handouts from organizations (e.g. voluntary organizations; local council; tourist boards; political parties) collected by the library
18–20	Blank cards for students to add their own thoughts.

Evaluation rationale

The approach is designed to throw light on which library services make any difference to students and why. This should enable students to convey whether and how they are functioning as independent learners and whether the library is recognized as encouraging this approach.

9.4.3 Structured focus groups

The main problem in working with groups is other people's time. You know what questions you want answered, but the people you want to talk to are usually busy and may not see library service development as their main concern – especially if they are generally happy with the service now on offer.

Participants in focus groups often complain that they don't have enough cohesion, or, in other words, the events lack sufficient structure to allow people to focus on the task in hand. The answer is to design and facilitate the activities carefully to help people give you the impact information you want.

You can overcome both these problems through the right choice of activity and a flexible approach. The people targeted for your questions may be busy but they probably come together in groups for meetings, education or training purposes. If so, the prospect of doing something a bit different may be intriguing.

Most evaluation calls for focus groups to be made up of various categories of potential service user; in other cases the expertise of the participants is at a premium.

- How easy is it to get a *representative group* together to focus on impact? This depends on whether people see your evaluation question as intrinsically interesting. If not, your best bet may be to link up with another activity that brings some or all of your target group together, or you may have to resort to offering incentives to participate. You may also wish to 'pick off' parts of your target group in different sessions if, for example, you want to involve high and low status people and if this difference is likely to get in the way of everybody contributing. However, choosing the right activities may remove the need for this type of separation.

- With *expert groups*, people will get involved if they see your topic as relevant and as a high enough priority (you will have to make the case and the initial approach carefully, explaining why they are the best people to get involved and what the benefits to them will be). A way forward is to identify one or more 'champions' who will be sufficiently interested in your evaluation to pave the way to other people. Setting up strategic focus groups requires a longer timescale to prepare the ground and to get into people's diaries.

9.4.4   Putting the spine into focus groups

The two key elements in running focus groups that work are setting up the conditions that enable people to concentrate on the job in hand and choosing the right activities. We have already said that good trainers will have a repertoire of structured activities to call upon. In talking to trainers about what you want it is important to remember the main difference between an evaluation focus group and a professional development event. Your main concern is to pick the brains of your participants rather than to give them a positive learning experience, although the two are not mutually exclusive.

A general rule for effective focus groups might be 'the less opportunity for unstructured discussion the better'. As to activities, options include brainstorming or card sort activities, as already described. In addition, you could try *small group generation of cartoons, diagrams, posters or bullet points* encapsulating their responses to carefully worded questions. As with card sorts, these provide opportunities for plenary exploration of issues, but there is also scope to get small groups to explain their ideas to each other (tape the discussions), or for them to write in sufficient detail for the next group to be able to understand and add to what the first group produced (doing your recording job for you). Unlike general discussions, all these activities will give you concrete impact information which has been fully endorsed by the participants.

Example 9.2   The short, sharp focus group

A series of short structured focus groups is used in a UK health service region as part of the review of its library services.

We target various groups of staff and consult administrators to find out where and when these people meet as part of their normal work. Then we contact the meeting convenors and ask for half an hour at their next meeting. The offer we make is that if they give us time to help review recent library service provision we will guarantee two things – we will finish within half an hour and people will find the activity interesting.

Steps:

1   Arrive with a set of 20–25 cards, each identifying a specific library service or aspect of provision, such as:

   • 'Ready access to photocopy facilities when studying/researching'

   or

   • 'Being able to browse contents pages of journals and request copies of articles of interest'.

2   Clear a table and position it so that people can stand round it. Explain the purpose and invite people to help identify where the library makes a difference and areas where it needs to have more impact.

   If the group size is appropriate (5–12 people):

- Deal out the cards to the participants as though they are playing cards.
- Explain that the table will be used to prioritize, with the top end as high success and the bottom as needing attention.
- Ask people individually (and all together) to put down 'their' cards anywhere on the table according to their view of its success.
- When this starts, tell them that they can put items above, below or beside cards that are already there but *not* move anything that is there.

This usually takes three or four minutes.

3 Now ask all the participants to look at the card layout and challenge anything that they think is placed too high or low by turning it face down. If anyone is unsure about what a card means (since they all consist of short phrases) they should turn it over too.

This usually takes another three to four minutes and results in about five to eight cards turned over. Record the remainder of the session (tape recorder or a colleague taking notes).

4 Starting at the top of the table, turn over the highest face-down item, read it out to the group and ask why it was turned over. You know that:

- someone wants an explanation – in which case ask the group what they think it means (*important:* don't offer your own explanation – you are there as an evaluator not as an expert); or
- there are at least two views about the relative importance of the item – invite a discussion and see if you can get a group consensus about where the item should be placed. If not, put it on one side and record that the group can't agree about it.

5 Continue working down the table until all the items are face up.

Through this process you lead a focused discussion about recent service impact, concentrating entirely on areas of difference or lack of understanding. The participants are equipped with a set of concepts through which to consider library service performance (probably for the first time ever). They agree on a ranking list of relative success, to which you can fairly easily assign scores so that you can compare results from different groups. They almost certainly find the activity interesting – and you have done the whole thing in half an hour or less. If the group finishes early, complete the task by asking them: 'If only one of these items can be addressed over the next three years, which should it be and why?'

9.5 Action research

What is action research? McKernan (1991) claims that:

Action research is carried out by practitioners seeking to improve their understanding of events, situations and problems so as to increase the effectiveness of their practice. Such research does not have the writing of research reports and other publications as a primary goal.

Action research aims at feeding the practical judgement of actors in problematic situations. The validity of the concepts, models and results it generates depends not so much on scientific tests of truth as on their utility in helping practitioners to act more effectively, skilfully and intelligently.

This is only one view of what can vary from cheap research conducted by practitioners dragooned into undertaking fieldwork on behalf of academic colleagues, through to real professional development based on the idea of the reflective practitioner focusing on service impact.

Action research makes the direct link between process and impact. It is essentially a cycle of reflecting, theorising and acting. The people involved move through stages. You

- identify a problem or challenge
- gather evidence
- then interpret this evidence together
- look for ideas on what changes to make
- make changes to the services
- then collect further evidence about the impact of these changes.

and so on until you feel that you have made enough progress.

Through action research, practitioners get evidence to discern what is happening at the moment and how well it is being received. This gives them scope to develop ideas about how to improve the situation and then turn them into new strategies and activities, which are evaluated in their turn. This cycle leads practitioners into exploring the different effects of various processes.

When it is done well, action research keeps practitioners focused on what they are trying to achieve. This approach should work in any library context; we have been able to see it working in various settings, from a semi-formal work group of health library managers to a formal impact evaluation programme involving 22 university library teams (Markless and Streatfield, 2005). Another instance is described below.

Action research is especially valuable when you are looking at 'messy' areas where there are no clear ways forward yet. With all the continuing developments in e-information, e-learning and information literacy work there is no shortage of such areas in libraries. The usual impact evaluation approach of comparing progress against a baseline starts to break down when the services provided to try to move on from the baseline are themselves changing and evolving rapidly. Action research enables you to engage in a rolling evaluation programme that accepts that yesterday's baseline is just history. With this approach you can change where you start from (your baseline) as well as where you are trying to get to (target) with each round of activity.

Since your rounds of activity are dictated by what you are finding out and wanting to change, they are not usually locked into the annual planning cycle – so it follows that your baseline and targets do not automatically tie in to any annual planning or reporting cycle. It is important to make this point if you are called upon to make an annual report on any action research programme that does not follow an annual cycle.

Example 9.3 Education librarians as action researchers

A small group of UK professionals (a school teacher, school librarians, further education lecturers and a college librarian) who recently completed their MA in Education discuss how they can continue to develop their practice. They want to keep up the momentum gathered during their Masters studies. The group feels that attending short staff development courses won't do: these tend to be too superficial. Reading may be interesting but won't necessarily galvanize the group into activity or provide the links between theory and practice that they want. They decide to set up an informal action research group and asked their MA tutor to facilitate termly meetings.

A year later, individuals in the group have:

* enhanced the after-hours support that they provide
* developed approaches to extended reading for adults with learning difficulties
* collaborated with colleagues to integrate the teaching of 'learning strategies' into subject courses
* enhanced the handling of groupwork differentiated according to the ability of the students in the college library.

The group meetings are held on Saturdays and attendance levels are high. Group members are clear that these improvements in their educational practice are due to adopting action research strategies.

Group members encourage each other to investigate aspects of their practice in a carefully structured and focused way; they read relevant research but are also supported while they question its relevance to their own contexts and develop their own ideas out about what they read. They use a variety of data-gathering techniques both in their initial investigations and when evaluating the impact of their changed practices. Group members openly report their difficulties and hold up their own development and their emerging ideas to critical scrutiny.

Despite working in difficult contexts, faced with increasing demands on their time and, in some cases, with decreasing budgets, engagement in action research has stopped group members from feeling powerless and de-professionalized. They are able to enhance the quality of their work in areas that they care about and in ways that accord with their educational values. Action research provided these practitioners with an effective tool for their own professional development and a way of improving the quality of education within their institutions. (Markless, 2003)

9.6   Doing it!

The actual evidence gathering is relatively straightforward, once you have decided what you want to collect and how. Don't forget that you are not the only people in the evidence collection business.

9.6.1 Getting help

Can you use partners to help you to collect evidence? Here are some ideas:

- If you want people to give you feedback about how resources are used by others, tell them what you would like them to look out for in advance, then ask for that information later (this is particularly important if you are asking busy teachers to help).
- Some strategic managers monitor impact evaluation developments; others write reports that may be useful if you can tap into them.
- Corporate performance monitoring teams in your wider organization may be collecting evidence themselves – can you 'ride on their coat tails' by getting them to ask questions that you want answered?
- Some people (librarians in your own and other sectors, booksellers? museums staff?) share some goals with your service and may be ready to collaborate over information gathering. Other libraries are likely to be looking at the same impact issues. Why not collaborate with them to produce better tools?
- Other people may have directly relevant evaluation expertise. For example, many trainers rely on the Kirkpatrick evaluation model, a four-level framework devised by Donald Kirkpatrick and presented in four journal articles published in 1959–60. This model has been the subject of a great deal of analysis and testing – any professional trainer is likely to have useful views on evaluation.

9.6.2   Practical difficulties in gathering evidence

There are some of the difficulties that crop up when service managers engage in evidence collection:

- Capturing evidence in *busy libraries* – this is the most common problem and it cannot be solved, but it can be managed. The problem affects both staff and users: if staff are really busy, any additional evidence collection is likely to be abandoned. From the user point of view, if your service is busy, users are less likely to want to be interrupted by your attempts to gather evidence. A careful balance is needed here – sometimes it is important to collect impact evidence of the service under stress; in other cases evidence from busy times is necessary to give the full picture. If you don't have to collect evidence at peak periods it obviously makes sense not to; where you have to, explaining to your staff and to users why it is necessary to do so and acknowledging that this creates problems should help you to get support.

- Unless you are collecting data on a large scale, impact evidence is different in kind from most traditional library evaluation data. Most impact evaluation involves using qualitative research methods where concerns such as getting a large enough sample of responses are less important than getting *robust evidence* that meets the resonance test (see section 8.4.3 in the previous chapter). This type of evidence is usually the best that is achievable, not, as is sometimes assumed, a poor second best. Getting this message across to people who are used to traditional busy-ness statistics may be hard work, but can be done.

- One pitfall is in the temptation to try to establish *cause and effect relationships* – this is *much* harder than it seems! We can learn something here from another field in which people struggle with demonstrating causal relationships and usually fail – education inspection. You may find it useful to adopt the approach and language of the UK education inspection teams, who look to see whether an activity is 'bearing upon' or is 'linked to' a service objective. A (positive or negative) link can be inferred if there is usually an improvement or decline in a situation when a specific service or activity is introduced or withdrawn.

- Whether you are asking people questions or observing them, it is important to behave in an *ethical* manner. Difficulties can arise if people don't know what you intend to do with the information they give you or don't like the questions you ask. (You should be safe if you follow our guidance in section 9.3.2.) They may also object to being observed. You can head off complaints by putting up a poster to say what you are doing and (in general terms) why. There are also hazards in collecting evidence from or about children. You may have to obtain prior permission from parents and the organization where you encounter the children may have specific rules about contact. If you have ever tried to photograph 22 children working with library materials when one of them has failed to bring the necessary parental authorization but keeps getting into the picture, you will know how frustrating these necessary rules can be.

- If you work in a health, social care or educational organization, there are likely to be protocols governing all research done there. You will need to check to see whether your evidence gathering falls within the organizational definition of research and, if so, how to get your activity cleared.

> **LAWS OF IMPACT EVALUATION 9**
> Effective impact work is not about gathering lots of evidence. It is about focusing on real impact and about rigour in collecting, analysing and reporting data.

9.7 Analysing data

We need to make a distinction here between quantitative data, which is usually fairly easy to organize into tables, and qualitative data, which is inherently more difficult to analyse. There are, of course, plenty of statistical packages and data analysis tools to help with this work. These tools range from the best known statistical aid, the Statistical

Package for the Social Sciences (SPSS)[1] to the new generation of data analysis tools. These newer tools can help in various ways, such as by giving easy access to data and extensive automation of clerical tasks at one extreme, or helping with qualitative analysis by combining 'subtle coding with qualitative linking, shaping, searching and modelling' at the other (e.g. NUD*IST and NVivo respectively).[2]

However helpful these tools are, and some of them are very helpful, there is no substitute for the evaluator developing a thorough understanding of the evidence. One effect of the widespread adoption of data analysis tools is that it is now too easy to do a superficial job of organizing the qualitative evidence and turning the results into a slick report. The reason why we advocate using qualitative methods to gather impact evidence is that this can give you subtle and nuanced evidence as well as powerful testimony in key areas. This can only be achieved if you do enough work with the qualitative evidence to really understand what it is telling you. Unless data analysis tools are used carefully they can get in the way of the real picture. If you are doing relatively small-scale qualitative evidence gathering, you may be better off cutting and pasting pieces of text and (physically or electronically) sorting and re-sorting them until useful patterns start to emerge. We still regard highlighter pens and scissors, as well as plastic or cardboard folders, as useful adjuncts to the evaluation data sense-making process.

When we referred to 'grounded theory' as an alternative to the hypothesis testing approach to research in section 2.4.1, we glossed over what many regard as the main contribution of Glaser and Strauss when proposing this approach – being systematic in analysing qualitative evidence. They identify three kinds of coding as being at the heart of their approach:

- open coding (the initial process of breaking down, analyzing, comparing and categorizing data – labelling, grouping and re-grouping incidents or events to form categories and properties)
- axial coding (teasing out hypothetical relationships between categories and sub-categories)
- selective coding (assembling the categories into the core category that becomes the basis of the grounded theory – which might be described as making sense of the data).

Interestingly, the two authors have since diverged in their approach, with Glaser challenging Strauss and his later collaborators (see Glaser, 1992) for, in his view, forcing data into a preconceived framework. Whether you choose to embrace grounded theory or not, it may be helpful to distinguish between these three types of coding, as well as to be wary about forcing your evidence into predetermined categories.

9.8   Interpreting and presenting your evidence

9.8.1   Another difficult area?

According to the respondents to Covey's (2002) survey of US academic libraries:

- Interpreting research findings is a particularly thorny problem, exacerbated when the data are imprecise or in conflict with other data or known trends, and when the research subjects are few or unrepresentative of the campus population.
- Even when evidence is carefully analysed and interpreted, managers may struggle with deciding how to organize and present it to an audience for consideration in decision making and strategic planning.

If you work systematically through the process described in this book you should not be faced with imprecise or conflicting impact evidence. By thinking carefully about who you want to get evidence from, and on how best to get that evidence, you should avoid getting your evidence from the wrong people. This leaves the question of how to present your evidence.

9.8.2   What is the main message?

When reporting findings it is tempting to follow the same sequence as in the interview schedule or questionnaire. This may work, if the original lines of questioning are logical and if they provide a coherent route through the evidence. The question to ask at this point is 'What are the most important findings from this evaluation?'. You may then have to change the way in which you report this evidence to get your message across.

9.8.3   Organize your findings

The key points to consider are:

- Who needs to know? Who do you want to influence with your impact evidence and who else has a right to know?
- Most people tend to take a 'one size fits all' approach to reports of evaluation findings. The usual pattern is start with as much evidence as you can put together, follow this with detailed conclusions and then add recommendations for action. What we know from much work on research dissemination is that this approach works for almost nobody. You need to ask how the key people you want to influence take their information on board. Even in these days of advanced e-communication, people find out a lot by talking to others. Can you boil down your key messages to a set of brief oral proposals and follow this up with an e-mail? Can you get a champion with influence in your organization to speak up for you instead? Is there a decision-making meeting to influence? If so, what is the ideal length and type of report?
- Assuming that you need to produce a written report, the guiding principle is – the shorter the better. Get your messages right. For strategic decision makers: try to put over your key findings on one page, with another page for recommendations for action. For operational managers: again offer key findings, show briefly how you reached them, and tailor your recommendations for action to that level. Make the evidence that informs your findings available for the few people who want it (as an appendix or on a website). Keep the raw evidence to compare it with next time – but don't

be tempted to show how much work you have done by circulating this.
• Ignore all these ground rules if they won't work in your organization!

Two final points:

• We said in the previous section that the UK education inspectors side-step the problem of cause and effect relationships when reporting their findings by using particular 'code words'. When they look at providing multimedia resources in schools and whether this changes anything, they report that it has

> a positive *bearing* upon differentiation (meeting individual pupil needs), motivating pupils, extending learning opportunities for pupils and cost-effective resource management.

They use qualitative evidence (drawn from such activities as lesson observation, interviews with teachers and scrutiny of lesson plans) when deciding whether schools are performing at a satisfactory level. Why not take a leaf from their book (or a word from their repertoire) when reporting your findings?
• We talk about impact evidence as being different in character from traditional library statistics, because it is usually gathered through social science research methods. If you use these methods it should be because you think they will tell you more about impact than traditional methods. If this is not what the people you report to are used to, you have an education job to do in persuading them that qualitative impact evidence is appropriate and, often, the best you can get. This will take time but it has to be done if you are to use such evidence for service accountability, resource negotiation or advocacy.

9.9   Sources on research methods

There are a number of more or less readable general publications on qualitative or quantitative research methods which are of use in evaluating the impact of libraries. Two works that we often recommend are Judith Bell's simple but sound introduction *Doing Your Research Project* written for the UK Open University (2005) and, for people who have a more specific focus, Robert K. Yin's *Case Study Research* (2002). If you want a more general round-up of how to design and manage library-focused research projects, Nick Moore's *How to Do Research* (2006) may help and there are other 'how to do it' guides available, such as Gorman and Clayton's *Qualitative Research for the Information Professional* (2004) or Ronald H. Powell and Lynn Connaway's *Basic Research Methods for Librarians* (2004).

If you would like to go into more depth about how to manage evidence, try Liz Orna's *Managing Information for Research* (1995).

9.10   Finding research methods e-resources

One area of the internet that has blossomed in recent years is the availability of good 'introductory through to expert' guidance material on all aspects of research methods, many of which are potentially useful when thinking about managing impact. Online books and journals, such as Mitchell and Jolley's *Research Design Explained* [3] or *Information Research* [4] e-journal are becoming more frequent and, fortunately, this growth has been accompanied by a burgeoning of websites offering guidance to what is available. Here, the range of potentially useful disciplines and methodologies comes into play: a quick round-up of useful sites covers:

- business research (US Academy of Management's RMWeb[5] website of the Research Methods Division)
- the social sciences generally (Research Resources in the Social Sciences,[6] including its own search engine)
- social research (Bill Trochim's Center for Social Research Methods,[7] or Resources for Methods in Evaluation and Social Research,[8] selected by two staff at the University of New York, Albany)
- information systems research (Qualitative Research in Information Systems[9] – a subsidiary site of *MIS Quarterly*, which claims to offer 'useful information on the conduct, evaluation and publication of qualitative research')
- educational research (offered by the BUBL[10] Gateway educational research section, which includes some research methods resources, for example covering action research)
- research methodologies (Kay Vandergrift's Research Methods on the World Wide Web,[11] offering 'sites selected because they address methodological issues and theories').

What about the library and information research methods fraternity? Continuing the pattern of useful websites being constructed by individuals we have Researching Librarian,[12] covering 'resources to assist librarians undertaking research' maintained by Kerry Smith at Mississippi State University. For the broader information services and systems field there is InformationR.net, covering information management, information science and information systems. This site offers access to a hugely valuable series of free Electronic Resources for Information Research Methods.[13]

For public libraries, the Counting on Results project funded by the Institute of Museum and Library Services in the USA is developing new tools for 'outcomes-based evaluation'.[14] This project looks at the impact of public libraries on individual patrons/users in six impact areas:

- basic literacy
- business and career information
- libraries as place
- information literacy
- local history and genealogy
- general information.

The same website gives access to the report on the research conducted to produce these materials (Lance et al., 2001).

For library managers interested in reader development, the Their Reading Futures[15] website has a batch of useful impact evaluation materials and the UK TeacherNet[16] website has an exhaustive 'tool kit' for evaluating the full range of school library services.

Finally, there are additional tools and materials linked to this book. To find them go to www.facetpublishing.co.uk/evaluatingimpact.

9.11   Evidence or advocacy?

There is one danger in how we go about collecting evidence and in looking at what it tells us. Even experienced researchers can get into a mess by confusing advocacy and evidence. When we started doing social science research, one of the best pieces of advice we received was to try to treat each new research situation as 'anthropologically strange'. To do this you start out by telling yourself that, however familiar a situation seems to be, you do not really know what is going on until you have gathered and looked carefully at the evidence. In other words, we should look at library services in the same way that a social anthropologist is expected to look at a group or tribe, by asking 'What appears to be going on here and how can I make any sense of it?'

Most of the time this doesn't create too many problems. If you have worked through the process so far, you should be ready to ask yourself what sorts of evidence will help to show the difference you are making. But evidence-based decision-making can rapidly degenerate into only picking evidence that will support a desired decision. Government bodies are especially likely to blur the distinction between service evaluation and advocacy – but they are not the only culprits, as our own experience shows.

Going back some years to the Effective School Library research project described in Chapter 3, we hit a problem when we reached the evidence analysis stage. Normally, there is a pattern to doing research, whether it is small-scale evaluation of a service or a large national project. After the initial energy buzz from getting the work started, you begin to get anxious (perhaps even depressed) when you see how much evidence is building up – will you ever make sense of it and will it tell you anything useful? Then, by the time you settle down to analyse the evidence and draw out the findings, the evidence speaks to you and the report writing or evidence presentation stage is usually straightforward.

When we reach this stage with the Effective School Library the evidence doesn't fit together. We start again but still can't make sense of what we are looking at. Then we start to think about *why* the analysis isn't working – and the answer suddenly becomes clear. Because we have worked for several years with school libraries we have unwittingly shifted from a research position to an advocacy stance. Everyone in the school library advocacy field at this time is busy calling for school libraries to be turned into learning resource centres designed to support students as independent learners'. (We now refer to this as the 'Holy Grail model' because it is a more or less distant aspiration that is unlikely to be fully achieved.) As we noted earlier, this approach is fine if the school as a whole is heavily committed to a student-centred approach to learning, but our research evidence clearly shows that this model of library provision won't work at all if the school puts a strong emphasis on traditional teaching. We want the Holy Grail model to work, but the evidence tells us something else.

As soon as we stop being hopeful advocates and turn back into realistic researchers it becomes clear that a different and more nuanced model is necessary to take account of the evidence that we have gathered. The evidence shows that schools differ in their approaches to teaching and learning and that what works well in supporting these vital activities in one school won't work at all somewhere else. The result is a 'horses for courses' approach to school library development that takes full account of where the school is now, what its teaching and learning priorities are and what level and type of library service can support these priorities. We learn important lessons in this project about the need to base development decisions on the research evidence about impact.

All of which brings us to our next 'law':

LAWS OF IMPACT EVALUATION 10
Beware of the Holy Grail! To gauge the impact of a service you need to know what change it is making, not what you hope it might do – evidence not aspirations.

We have deliberately not suggested any specific activities (or steps) for you in this chapter because the whole focus is on you doing it!

Notes

1   www.spss.com/worldwide/
2   www.qsrinternational.com/software.htm
3   http://spsp.darion.edu/mm/RDE3/
4   http://informationr.net/ir/
5   www.aom.pace.edu/rmd/
6   www.researchresources.net
7   http://trochim.human.cornell.edu/
8   http://gsociology.icaap.org/methods/
9   http://misq.org/misqd961/isworld
10   http://bubl.ac.uk/link/e/educationalresearch.html
11   www.scils.rutgers.edu/~kvander/researchmethods.html
12   www.mstate.edu/~kerjsmit/trl
13   http://informationr.net/rm/
14   www.lrs.org/CoR.asp
15   www.theirreadingfutures.org.uk/
16   www.teachernet.gov.uk/schoollibraries

10

Taking stock, setting targets and development planning

This chapter starts by looking at how to review the impact indicators generated through the process in order to keep the whole thing manageable! We then focus on setting realistic impact targets and conclude by considering where and how development planning fits into the process of evaluating impact.

10.1 Taking stock: reviewing your impact and process indicators

Before you move on to select your targets, it will be useful to stop and review all your impact indicators. There are four main dimensions:

- **Range**. Do your indicators reflect the full range of what you are trying to change *and* give you enough of a picture of whether your services are working efficiently?
- **Number**. Have you generated too many indicators? Publications on managing performance usually recommend 15–20 'key' indicators (including both process and impact indicators), with any others considered as secondary. If you go much beyond that scale it becomes difficult to gain and retain an overall picture of what is going on. Too many indicators can also lead to diverting over much energy into collecting evidence rather than running your service.
- **Relevance**. Do all the indicators really tell you something useful and contribute to the overall picture? Are you still collecting 'traditional' performance data because you have always done so? Are any of your indicators only used as the basis for making management reports?
- **User focus/service focus**. Do you have a balance between 'outward looking' user-focused indicators and 'inward looking' system enhancement indicators?

No matter how much care you take in writing and reviewing your indicators, they may not all work. All indicators ought to be regarded as provisional at the outset. They should be monitored to see if they are leading you to really useful information. If not, change them or ditch them.

10.2 Setting targets for impact

Impact targets aim at improving the effectiveness of the service; they focus on discernible differences in impact on people in significant areas of use of the service. They are different from process targets, which record what people have done. Impact targets can be concerned with the whole community served or parts of it.

See also the definitions offered in 'Impact and all that: use of some key terms in this book' on page xiii.

10.2.1 Baseline information, what baseline information?

Whenever we work through this model with library service managers, we have to stop at this point. The reason is that when service managers look closely at what they want to achieve and at the sort of evidence that will tell you whether you are getting there, you usually do not have the baseline information about where you are now that will enable you to set sensible targets (e.g. What proportion of your current ICT users are unemployed or elderly? What proportion of health workers are effective information users? How many members of reading groups are avid readers when they join a group?).

When we work as consultants to help a management team to work through the process, there is usually a pause of several months at this stage so that people can go off and assemble baseline information. If you set targets without sufficient baseline information you are guessing in the dark. You are also potentially setting yourself up to fail.

10.2.2 Writing impact targets

You are now in a position to consider setting realistic but challenging targets: you know how the service is currently performing in key areas (baseline data collected on your impact and process indicators) and you know where you would like to be. However, quantifying the improvements you want can be difficult – and target setting should not be about 'plucking figures out of the air'. Your targets should be sufficiently challenging to stretch the service but not so far out of reach as to be demotivating.

When setting targets it may be helpful to consider target zones. A study for the National Foundation for Educational Research in England and Wales (Arnold, 1998) sums up the idea of target zones clearly:

- *The historic zone.* Targets in this zone are those that are *behind* current performance, which is hidden to the extent that others are not aware of its quality. By this means, standstill can be represented as improvement – it is a means of 'domesticating' any threats that targets may offer.
- *The comfort zone.* Targets in this zone seek to keep improvement very much within reach. They often reflect a belief that there is really no need to improve.
- *The smart zone.* Targets in this zone are sufficiently ahead of the present state of play to make a difference.
- *The unlikely zone.* Targets in this zone seek large improvements through 'determination and high aspiration, or recklessness'. They can be a recipe for high risk and high stress.

It needs no guesswork to arrive at which of these zones is the ideal, although in practice library services show very different aspirations in their target setting.

Impact targets lend themselves to more precise quantification than process targets and are nearly always expressed as a quantity or proportion.

The wording of the targets should not be too difficult if you are happy with your indicators. Whereas an indicator is couched in terms of:

- the number of staff confident to . . .
- the number of staff with knowledge of . . .
- the proportion of schools satisfied with . . .
- the number of unemployed people/retired people/teenagers using . . . ,

the targets state what specific improvement is being aimed at:

- 5% more managers are satisfied with the quality of communication with library staff, compared with the previous year
- 90% of participants in user training focused on internet searching report that they are now more confident when conducting searches
- 30% of partner organizations have a better understanding of the contribution of the library service to their joint work.

Occasionally, it may be possible to set targets without including a 'target figure' (if, for example, you aspire to generate a love of books among a particular group of people). However, there is no point in setting targets unless you have some way of finding out when you have reached the level of success at which you are aiming. This can be achieved by other means, such as a thorough and systematic qualitative research study focused in the target area – but this is likely to be more lengthy and resource-dependent than impact evaluation against quantitative targets.

Your targets should specify the time-period over which they are to be met (usually one year, or three to five years in a strategic plan). Do not automatically try to fit your impact target cycle into your annual planning cycle – they may not fit! As one service manager said:

> The trouble with national audit indicators is that they are all geared to the annual financial cycle. Impact does not occur to fit the annual cycle and has to be viewed over a longer term.

10.2.3 Some issues

- You may find it helpful to consult any available benchmarking information (see section 11.6) when you consider the level at which to set targets. How are similar services performing? There may also be clues about achievable levels in the results of national/federal/state research.

- It is easy to wander into fantasy land when setting targets if you don't take full account of the existing resources available to deliver and the competing priorities within your service. You may want to have much greater impact in a particular area of work, but over-committing your resources in a particular area may lead to unwelcome distortion of the service or to missed targets.
- If too many impact targets are adopted at the same time this will lead to failure, because too many targets will cause confusion rather than concentrate effort. Each impact target is likely to drag a raft of process targets along in its wake, because you have to do things to meet targets and will probably want to ensure that these are done.
- Targets are not always about 'more of . . .'. You may deliberately set targets that maintain current levels of impact or, in some cases, choose a lower level of impact (e.g. if the user group or its expectations have changed).

10.2.4 The target snare

The trouble with targets is that as soon as you focus on them they start to have a distorting effect. This phenomenon is well stated by Marilyn Strathern (1997), who draws on what is known as Goodhart's Law by asserting that 'When a measure becomes a target it ceases to be a good measure.' The original version of this Law is a bit more convoluted; as stated by Charles Goodhart (1983), one time Chief Adviser to the Bank of England: 'Any observed statistical regularity will tend to collapse once pressure is placed on it for control purposes.'

How can this conundrum be solved? The best that we can hope to do is to remember that targets are not sacrosanct; they have been chosen by managers for a specific purpose and are only useful as long as they help – in this case, as long as they help you to improve the service.

> **LAWS OF IMPACT EVALUATION 11**
> If impact targets are not helping, change them or ditch them.

10.2.5 Imposed targets

So far, we have assumed that you are interested in setting targets for the active development of your service. However, we have to acknowledge that there is an increasing tendency for targets to be imposed from above (e.g. in the UK, improvements in literacy, and public access to ICT in libraries are both government-driven). It is important to recognize that imposed targets are usually prescribed as a control mechanism by government. As a result, such targets tend to be very general, arbitrary and subject to abandonment or change as political circumstances warrant. Service managers usually have to subscribe to imposed targets, but we believe that it is also important to persist with more appropriate development-driven targets in our rapidly changing world. As Carol Taylor Fitz-Gibbon (1996) observes:

The imposition of targets or the development of ossified plans is not the approach which seems to fit best with the ideas of complex systems thriving in a region of complexity on the edge of chaos.

She may be talking about schools rather than libraries but the description seems highly appropriate for libraries in the 21st century!

Targets can also be imposed by the larger organization of which the library service is part (e.g. pharmaceutical companies usually have a strong information agenda; local/state authorities have their own priorities too!). Although such targets are likely to feel less distant, it may be problematic to embrace corporate targets wholesale. Targets that are not 'owned' (or at least influenced) by the people who have to meet them can alienate more than motivate. It is not surprising that imposed targets are sometimes called 'in-house terrorists' – they can spread panic and discontent!

10.3 Process targets

Process targets are concerned with changes in what the service does and how. Planning tends to be dominated by process targets in much the same way that services generate a lot of process indicators and hardly any impact indicators. However, you will always use more process targets than impact ones; and indeed it is a mistake to adopt too many impact targets because each one inevitably drags related process targets along in its wake.

We tend to write process targets in one of two ways:

- Focus on task completion – e.g. you may decide to develop a new stock selection procedure or to put new monitoring/data collection mechanisms in place.
- Focus on increased or decreased activity – e.g. attend 20% more curriculum meetings; consult 10% more non-users of the service.

10.4 Development planning

It may be a little disingenuous to claim that once you have worked through this model the development plan writes itself. However, it should now be a much less difficult task to express the initial aims and processes as time-limited and specific objectives linked to realistic targets, and to be confident of knowing when the service has achieved what it set out to do.

Our model offers a framework for strategic and service level planning. If it works, it will help you form a clear view of what you want to achieve, and support your exploration of the processes that should help you get there. Using the model then leads you to collect the data that will tell you how you are currently performing in each key area. With all this information you should be ready to plan effectively. If you work through our model you will come to the development plan in its proper place – at the *end* of the planning process. This makes the development plan more meaningful, not just a document based on 'historic fiction plus 5%'.

Further points:

- There is a difference between *maintenance and development*. Most development plans that we have seen present managers with a mass of activities and targets all labelled 'development'. This makes 'real' development very difficult; you can end up engaged in lots of activity but with little sense of getting anywhere. You will need to make choices about which areas of work should be maintained (which could be linked to a set of maintenance targets or standards) and in which areas the service should try to move forward. The baseline data that you collect to illuminate your current impact and performance, will help in this work.

  This distinction can be empowering in itself, giving a renewed sense of purpose. If you separate maintenance from development, you can identify how much resource will be 'used up' in maintaining essential services and infrastructure, and how much spare capacity will then be available to support development activities.
- The basic constraint for librarians is having to spend so much time on managing and operating the library infrastructure. This means that you probably do most development work 'at the margins', at least in the early stages of the work (unless additional development funding can be secured). One characteristic of successful initiatives is that they become part of the normal work over time ('the institutionalization stage' in educational change-speak); occasionally an initiative may lead to the library operating differently, but this is unusual and is in any case likely to take around five years to achieve.
- You will have to *prioritize*. Inevitably you will not be able to do all that you want to immediately. You will need to decide on criteria for prioritising (for example, focusing on where the library is supporting corporate priorities, or government initiatives, or deciding to tackle areas of 'worst' performance).
- Development planning should lead directly to more detailed *action planning*. Many development plans are not implemented because they are left at too high a level (not nailed down to the practicalities of implementation). Once you have decided what key changes are necessary to ensure the development of the library service and what your targets are, you will need to plan the tasks required to implement these changes. You should try to ensure that:

— key tasks are defined and understood
— necessary actions are listed
— accountabilities for each action are defined and accepted
— performance targets are set for each action
— performance measures for each action are identified and documented
— mechanisms are in place to review the achievement of targets and to feed the review
  into future planning activities
— timescales for each activity are set.

(based on Kinnell, Usherwood and Jones, 1999a)

10.5 Planning your impact evaluation

10.5.1 Some challenges

In looking at US university library attempts to evaluate their services, Covey (2002) listed some of the pitfalls in managing evaluation:

> Respondents reported frequent breakdowns in the research process because of inadequate planning, particularly in scheduling and marshalling the resources needed to complete the project. Poor planning created problems that cascaded through the . . . process and, when compounded by inadequate skills, doomed it to failure or only partial success.
>
> They focused on the resources needed to gather, analyse, and perhaps interpret the data. Resources needed to manage the project and complete the process – to document and present the findings, develop plans to use them, and implement the plans – were not addressed at the same level of detail.
>
> Limited resources typically restricted implementation to solving only the problems that were cheap and easy to fix.
>
> The picture they painted is not a picture of a culture of assessment or of an organization in which assessment is a core activity crucial to the library's mission.

10.5.2 Meeting these challenges?

If you are undertaking a significant amount of impact evaluation work, this will have to be carefully planned. As the Covey comments show, it is easy to overlook or under-prepare aspects of this work. You may find it useful to look at the planning checklist provided as part of the Inspiring Learning for All (www.inspiringlearningfor all.gov.uk) programme (see section 6.9.1).

This is what it involves:

- debating what you mean by learning in the context of your museum, archive or library
- setting up a team to lead the process
- auditing your service provision using the Inspiring Learning for All checklists to identify your strengths and areas to improve
- identifying evidence to demonstrate that you meet the stated goals of Inspiring Learning for All and deciding where there are gaps in your evidence
- developing an action plan to improve your services and overall support for learners
- assessing learning outcomes for users; for this you can use the generic learning outcome system which is fully explained in the 'Measure

Learning' section of the website; the evidence of learning outcomes that you collect will feed in to your action planning and support your advocacy work

- developing a convincing case and an advocacy strategy that will help you to win support for learning both internally and externally
- feeding this back to develop individuals, teams and your organization.

Part 3
Back to the issues

11

Where do we go from here?

> This chapter moves beyond the practical aspects of impact evaluation covered so far. It puts a toe in the water by introducing some issues and offers further sources to take up if you are interested in finding out more.
>
> What else do you need to think about if you want to take impact evaluation seriously? Evaluation can be too narrow, too shallow, too short term or undertaken too soon. We discuss these concerns below and then look at the scope for benchmarking around impact and at where all this work fits into the move towards evidence-based library work.

11.1 Getting impact evaluation right

The process introduced in the main part of this book is intended to be practical and to meet the immediate impact evaluation needs of library service managers looking at accountability or seeking to develop their services. To keep things as straightforward as possible, we have concentrated on evaluating the impact of parts of your service, especially those parts where you are trying to make a real difference to specific target groups of users or potential users. We have tried to take account of the unprecedented major change that is going on in the library world especially in relation to electronic service provision and information literacy.

Even so, there is a danger that impact evaluation carried out by service managers can miss important parts of the picture. In particular, there is a risk that impact evaluation can be too narrow in its focus (so that the big picture is missed), too shallow in its execution, too short term (getting instant feedback can be easy but may also be very misleading), and it may miss important change altogether if it is done too soon. How can we avoid these potholes?

11.2 Getting beyond the narrow focus

11.2.1 Social capital

How can we look at the big questions about how libraries contribute to the cohesion and development of their communities or organizations? One way of exploring this theme is through the concept of social capital – defined as the stock of active connections among people in a community, or the trust, mutual understanding, and shared values and behaviours that bind the members of human networks and communities and make co-operative action possible (Cohen and Prusak, 2001). According to the World Bank (1999) social capital is not just the sum of the institutions which underpin a society – it is the glue that holds them together.

The basic premise is that interaction enables people to build communities, to commit themselves to each other, and to knit the social fabric. Developing a sense of belonging and getting involved in social networks can, it is claimed, bring great benefits to people, partly through the relationships of trust and tolerance that evolve (Smith, 2001). Without this interaction, on the other hand, trust decays; and eventually begins to manifest itself in serious social problems (Beem, 1999).

Evaluation of social capital focuses on the density of social networks that people are involved in; the extent to which they are engaged with others in informal, social activities; and their membership of groups and associations. A key dimension of social capital is whether interaction is *bonding* (exclusive) or *bridging* (inclusive). The former is more inward looking and may reinforce exclusive identities and homogeneous groups. The latter is more outward-looking and may encompass people across different social divides (Putnam 2000).

Although the concept of social capital can readily be applied to communities, it is now being explored with firms and organizations (Cohen and Prusak, 2001) as people become

> increasingly suspicious of the 'people, processes, technology' mantra, 'ceaselessly intoned as a summary of the sources of organizational effectiveness' (8).

Interestingly, the organizational benefits claimed include better knowledge sharing, due to established trust relationships, common frames of reference and shared goals.

Libraries of all kinds have the potential to contribute to the development of social capital. The concept has not so far been widely applied to libraries and their impact, but the scope for this sort of approach is being explored, notably by Alan Bundy (2003a; 2003b) and Anne Goulding (2004). If you are sufficiently interested to explore the possibilities of social capital as a focus for library impact evaluation, Kathleen Swinbourne (2000) offers advice on conducting your own social capital audit (based on experience in Australian public libraries).

11.2.2 The social impact audit

This approach offers another way into social-capital-focused evaluation. It has been adopted in the library world by Rebecca Linley and Bob Usherwood (1998) to help garner qualitative information in a context where

> The [Government] is only concerned with what is measurable and, as a result, tends to ignore a great deal of what is important.

The social impact audit offers a 'tool for enabling sensible measurement of complex outcomes' and a 'technique that makes the enacting process (of libraries) visible'. It is a qualitative technique, but one that, the authors argue, is none the less legitimate and rigorous.

In essence, the social impact audit is a way to explore whether and in what ways your services have impact on key social areas such as encouraging economic regeneration, enhancing the health of the community, reducing anti-social behaviour or increasing a sense of community. In other words the approach allows you to look at the impact of your services in ways that go beyond the effect on individuals. An interesting aspect of this approach is that when people are asked to think about these bigger impact questions they usually struggle to connect and then frequently come up with surprising and revealing replies. (In one community, the library is identified as the only public building that is not vandalized and various reasons are offered for this. Elsewhere, specific services provided by the library make it one of a cluster of local attractions seen as bringing in tourists and visitors from the surrounding area.)

Linley and Usherwood acknowledge that, as with many qualitative techniques, the social impact audit is time consuming and hard to formulate. However, if the alternative is not having clear evidence of the contribution of the service to individuals and to the community, the service will be judged on limited information that significantly underplays its value.

The process is based on extensive and carefully focused 'discussions' with stakeholders – all of whom are to be identified to obtain 'as full a view as possible of the social aspects of public library activity'. The 'discussions' take place using interviews, focus groups and workshops. Community profiling enables stakeholders to be identified and valid focus groups to be constructed.

The authors claimed that the social impact audit obtains 'real world data' in a 'rigorous way'. It is qualitative data but is promoted as 'valid evidence and – should be treated as such by politicians and professionals alike' (85).

The social impact audit offers a positive way of looking at the bigger picture of the impact of public library services on their communities. There is also potential for using this approach in other settings such as academic communities. It is an open question whether the social impact audit is really a technique (as Linley and Usherwood assert) or a helpful framework in which to do impact evaluation work. Either way, if you adopt this approach it should help you to maintain attention on the broader impact issues for your service.

11.3   Digging deeper

Our model of impact evaluation should work if you can establish what sort of impact your service is having now and have some feel for what sort of impact it is likely to have one, three or five years hence. Problems arise if the programme that you want to evaluate is inherently innovatory, unpredictable or plain messy. As libraries of all kinds extend the possibilities of electronic information provision or go beyond familiar ways of delivering services, it is sometimes difficult to gauge what sort of impact services should be having, because there are no meaningful precedents.

To give an example, when a consortium of university libraries asks whether their joint cataloguing of e-resources (aimed at enhanced access by all kinds of higher education users) is having sufficient effect to justify further joint funding – the short answer is that they don't know enough to begin to predict likely impact over the next few years. Will regionally based resource discovery collaboration be redundant next year or within five years as search engine providers become more ambitious? Current evaluation criteria for this type of service are probably too heavily rooted in past traditions of study and research to be of much use. In this as in other areas where libraries are looking at and doing new things it may take time for evaluation to catch up, or we may have to think about how to evaluate in different ways.

To push this issue further, most approaches to evaluation (possibly including our own) expose service managers to the danger of sliding into utilitarian rationalism – omitting any place for imagination. You can't always specify appropriate objectives at the outset (although this is the first step in our approach). Even so, you may want to try something because it feels like a good idea or in response to a complex problem where you think your solution just might fit. This is fine – if you have the spare capacity to pursue it. This is not an argument for jettisoning evaluation altogether. In fact, it is probably more important to evaluate the impact of these sorts of initiatives because they offer the prospect of dramatic improvement if they work. It is also important to evaluate the impact of initiatives that take time, energy and effort away from keeping the system working (moving beyond infrastructure maintenance) because this effort is inevitably using up precious time squeezed out from the thousand and three things that you have to do to keep the system functioning adequately. You need to know whether your innovation is paying off, as soon as you have worked out how.

These difficulties may be relatively new for the library service impact evaluation arena, but other disciplines have been trying to find ways of evaluating messy and evolving innovations for years. To take a leaf from an educational evaluation book, if your programme:

- has complex goals that are difficult to define precisely
- is dominated by 'special' influences, such as the particular character of the institution

or

- there is insufficient time, a paucity of standard data or uncertainty about what evaluation questions to ask (so that formalized evaluation designs are inappropriate)

then illuminative evaluation is probably the answer – at least so two of its main proponents Malcolm Parlett and Garry Dearden (1977) claim. We have already outlined this approach (section 2.4.2) but commend it again here because it:

- gets past the need to specify objectives in advance
- allows you to engage with evaluation even when likely outcomes are hazy
- through the idea of progressive focusing, enables you to concentrate more and more on what emerges as important as you go along.

11.4 Looking long enough

Since most library services are more or less locked into an annual planning cycle and have only limited time to do evaluation, it is not surprising that much evaluation tends to be too short term and superficial to really pick up on impact.

11.4.1 Getting beyond the reactionnaire

The classic post-event questionnaire used to get feedback at the end of most training events is of some use to event managers (to monitor whether participants have a good time, strongly dislike the idiosyncrasies of a trainer, or enjoy the food provided), which is why they are sometimes called reactionnaires. They are of little use in telling you whether the event is effective as an educational opportunity because they are administered too soon after the event for any learning or growth in confidence to be detected or for any enhanced skills or knowledge to be applied. It is feasible to get more useful impact evidence by following up with a selection of participants two or three months after the event to ask what they remember from the experience, whether they feel more confident as a result, what they have applied in their work since or what they have otherwise drawn upon, but this is more expensive than collecting reactionnaires.

11.4.2 Premature evaluation

The follow-up interview may do a better job than the reactionnaire in getting at the impact of training events, but in asking about the impact of specific educational experiences we are in danger of over-simplifying a complex process. Race (2005) pointed to the dangers of pre-specifying educational targets and learning outcomes:

> In our target driven systems of post-compulsory education, there seems little room for 'Not-yet-successful learning' . . . the most complex ideas probably need to be grasped and lost several times before they are gradually retained more permanently and safely.

Significant changes in people's behaviour may take a long time to get established. A lawyer may accept the argument for undertaking systematic database searches when working with clients, or a clinician might recognize the need to become more evidence-based in treatment decisions. It may still take months or even years, with follow-up support along the way, before this shift is translated into significant change in how they do their day-to-day work, if this happens at all.

Which of our programme evaluations is sufficiently flexible to pick up on this sort of learning? If you really want to find out the long-term effects of your interventions, it is necessary to think about evidence gathering months or years beyond the initial engagement and about using methods (such as the critical incident interview) that help respondents to identify the effects of your work long after the event.

11.4.3 Choose a longer time-frame

We have already said that the one year planning cycle becomes an encumbrance if your innovation is complex and the outcomes are problematic. A variation on this theme that crops up in most libraries is the need for dust to settle after restructuring or reorganization. Your impact indicators may not work as well after the changes as before and may now be irrelevant. But since you can't be sure how the newly configured service is bedding down, a short interregnum is probably a good idea, before you decide on your success criteria and targets, once the managers have some experience of the new structures and ways of working.

To give two examples of current structural changes in public library services in the UK, many public library service points are now being realigned as front-line service points incorporating a range of other user services offered by local authorities (such as housing advice or even marriage registration). Similarly, some local authority children's library services are being incorporated within a wider range of education, social and health care services to children, with even the senior managers involved unclear about how the new service will fit together and operate. In both these instances, to judge the public library service impact in isolation makes no sense, but what difference will the converged services make to the library part of the new service and how will the library services change in response? Only time will tell – common sense suggests that impact targets should be suspended until the new service is properly in place.

In higher education, similar issues are encountered around convergence of libraries and other learning support services. Again, it makes sense to wait and look at impact when managers have some idea of realistic expectations for the new service.

11.5 Getting help

The aim of this book is to enable you to undertake impact evaluation of your library service. However, we recognize that this may involve other people (such as members of your work team) and that not everyone takes naturally to evaluation work. When are they likely to need help and what sorts of help? Dorothy Williams and her colleagues (2005) looked at impact evaluation support needs in a small survey carried out as a follow-up to their review of the available evidence about social, learning and economic impacts of museums, archives and libraries considered earlier (section 3.2). They found that:

The respondents appeared to fall into two groups: those embarking on impact evaluation with limited experience who wanted help in the form of practical tools and examples of techniques and instruments, and those with greater understanding of the issues who viewed the resources in terms of maintaining professional awareness, keeping up to date and being provided with pointers to relevant resources outwith their normal professional sources of information. (546)

We hope that the suggestions in this book will move people beyond this set of problems. But what sorts of support are likely to be needed in undertaking the evaluation process described in this book? The first ten university library teams who adopted this general approach as the core of the action research programme referred to earlier (section 3.5.2) identified several practical problems in doing evaluation (Markless and Streatfield, 2006). They came up with three clusters of problems, which can be approached in different ways. Although these teams all work in academic libraries, the pattern of useful support is similar across the board.

11.5.1 Problems in managing the impact evaluation process

Most of these problems amount to variations on the usual issues in managing competing priorities and trying to move the service forward:

- what to prioritize and where to start, given the other competing demands on library management time
- conflict in timescales between the reporting needs of the service and the natural evidence-collection cycle for an initiative
- the cost of commercial software (affecting the thrust to digitize as well as access to e-information)
- how to organize appropriate professional development so that library colleagues can help to collect reliable evidence
- understanding current innovations in teaching and learning and how they affect library service provision.

If you are looking for outside help in these areas you should be able to find people who know their way around current ideas on managing change and who are skilled in facilitating this aspect of professional development. (A useful collection of support materials, originally commissioned by the People's Network Programme to help public libraries to move into e-working, can be found at www.mla.gov.uk/action/pn/change.asp).

Other management problems seem to be specific to impact evaluation:

- how to isolate the library contribution to joint initiatives (getting collaborators to comment on the effect of the library contribution)

- how to defend choices of research methods (particularly when reporting to academic colleagues, many of whom specialize in aspects of research)
- research design issues:

  — devising questionnaires to test the skills you want to test
  — screening out library/academic jargon through adequate piloting
  — how to collect 'unadulterated' evidence, given the vested interests of those involved
  — choosing a timescale and timing that will take account of key features in the academic year.

However, all of these difficulties are regularly encountered by anyone managing social science research projects and this is the direction to look in if you want external help. These are also problems where a small amount of expert advice is likely to be a big help.

11.5.2 Practical research issues

Again, we are in the territory of the social science researcher. We have cheated here by offering ways forward [in parentheses] after listing the problem, in case you run up against the same problem and would like a quick answer:

- how to overcome the tendency for respondents (e.g. academics/researchers) to tell you what they *should* be doing [ask them to choose from paragraphs giving vignettes/scenarios based on real practice, then to modify them by changing words, to make a closer fit to their own behaviour]
- what to do if users fail to recognize their information literacy limitations [timing is important: e.g. new students have no clear idea of what is expected of them at the beginning of a course of study]
- how to focus on use of websites when users may not know which sites they have used [try interviewing users while they are searching]
- how to deal with unresponsive/defensive/lying interview respondents [look for training in research interview technique]
- how to get feedback from academic staff when they mark student assignments that involve library use [brief them on what evidence you want before they do the marking, then contact them straight afterwards to get feedback].

What external help to look for here depends upon the amount of help that you need. Universities that offer courses in library and information studies should have staff who are experienced in qualitative research and who can facilitate groupwork for all types of libraries. They may also be able to offer help in evaluating the impact of aspects of your work (such as information literacy support) directly or by deploying students to do practical research in their dissertations. Using students is most effective if you are able and ready to give time to ensure that their evaluation approach and focus produces evidence that can help your library to develop. University faculties of education or departments of teaching and learning have staff who are experienced in evaluating educational interventions. Better yet, if they have the will, academic staff can collaborate creatively with library service managers and their staff to produce better evaluation, as described by Harada (2005).

11.5.3 Help in conducting action research

If you decide to adopt an action research approach, the key to any outside help is good facilitation. External facilitators need to choose carefully the nature of the support role at each stage in the process and be ready to act accordingly. They need a range of research, change management and facilitation skills to support this type of development activity (see Markless and Streatfield, 2006).

11.6 Towards impact benchmarking

When you have gathered your impact evidence you should be able to compare (or benchmark) the impact of your services with those of other people. Or should you? Before we look at the possibilities for this kind of comparison, what do we mean by benchmarking and how well is it done in the more traditional library service monitoring areas?

11.6.1 Output and process benchmarking

We commonly encounter two types of service benchmarking:

- **output** (or data) **benchmarking** – in which you relate the inputs (resources) to the outputs of a defined aspect of your service with one or more library services elsewhere. (For example, you can look at the direct purchase costs of loan materials in relation to the total loans in a given year.) It is fairly easy to achieve these sorts of comparisons, providing that you and the other managers involved define all your terms consistently and measure them equally accurately in each library (e.g. who exactly are included as 'users'?). You will also have to think about the underlying assumptions in such comparisons (in this case, that cheaper loans are better).
- **process benchmarking** – in which you look at what you do with the inputs to try to achieve specific outputs (ways of using resources to get particular effects). If you do process benchmarking with other library services, this offers some basis for comparing what processes are undertaken and how (e.g. between the point when a book is selected for purchase and its first loan). However, you again need to think about assumptions. (Is the simplest or cheapest set of processes automatically the best?) To be effective, you should conduct benchmarking with similar services (in size, state of development and aims) and get into discussion with the managers of the other services about any identified differences, to find out why they occur.

The common denominator between these two approaches is that you undertake them in an attempt to improve the quality of the services under review, or to provide a basis for organizational/federal/government service monitoring.

To introduce another layer of complexity, advocates of both output and process benchmarking commonly urge managers to make comparisons with the best comparable organizations in any sector – not just libraries. Output benchmarking, in particular, can rapidly degenerate into a control instrument for government agencies, ensuring that organizations commit disproportionate resources to outperforming their peers in narrowly prescribed areas and, in doing so, demonstrate that the service (or the government) is meeting more or less arbitrary improvement targets.

On a more positive note, outcomes-focused process benchmarking appears to be growing in popularity. For example, although Larry Brady of FMC, one of the biggest US corporations (quoted by Kaplan and Norton, 1993), is scathing about most output benchmarking, he is a strong advocate of process benchmarking:

> We ask our managers to go outside the organisation and determine the approaches that will allow achievement of their long-term targets . . . we want to stimulate thought about how to do things differently to achieve the target rather than how to do existing things better.

Taking this argument a step further, if we want to do things differently, it is important to know about the impact of what we are doing now, which brings us to the idea of benchmarking around impact.

11.6.2 The scope for impact benchmarking

In case you think we are taking a short flight into cloud cuckoo-land, we are not alone in thinking about impact benchmarking. In the United Kingdom, various parts of the central government (notably the Cabinet Office, the Treasury, the National Audit Office and the NHS Executive) are showing great interest in the prospect of benchmarking on the basis of impact and achievement (QMW, 1999). However, they all acknowledge that nobody is doing it well – yet! This is not to say that it cannot be done.

11.6.3 Doing impact benchmarking

In order to benchmark around impact you need to be able to compare evidence of the impact of specific services directly with those in another library, as a starting point for thinking about how to deliver better services. As with process benchmarking, this works best if the organizations are similar in size and state of development, but such similarities are not enough. Our work has shown that even when libraries are doing roughly the same things (for example, designing and delivering critical appraisal skills workshops for hospital clinicians) their objectives and targets may well be different. Unless you limit your choice to 'like-minded' library services, you will have to take account of such differences when interpreting relative strength of impact.

There may, of course, be all sorts of reasons why one service has more impact than another, so it is also important to reduce the possibilities. The ideal here is to be able to compare the impacts of a particular service provided in two or more settings in which the same things are done in broadly the same way over a similar time period. It is equally important to use the same evidence-gathering instruments applied in the same way and at the same time. Ideally, you need toolkits of assessment instruments on which to draw (e.g. questionnaires or interview schedules), as well as precise and fully documented descriptions of the processes undertaken to achieve the impact in each setting, so that any subtle differences can be identified.

One of the keys to successful benchmarking is to do it at the right time. You will be ready for benchmarking *after* you have systematically worked out your service objectives and priorities. This should help in focusing on things that other people are doing that you might not otherwise think about. If benchmarking is started too early it may push you into someone else's agenda and solutions – you may get hooked into their outputs and processes which may not achieve the impact you want.

Is impact benchmarking with organizations other than libraries feasible? Probably not, at this stage. In principle, it should be possible to make meaningful comparisons with specific services offered by other carefully selected organizations. But whether the amount of necessary exploration of the differences between the work environments and organizational drivers is likely to be worthwhile in terms of lessons learnt through the comparisons is highly questionable.

The idea of impact benchmarking across public services of specific types is creeping up federal/government agendas. Perhaps fortunately, national or regional comparisons of service impact are difficult to achieve, as work in the schools evaluation field has amply demonstrated. It is no real surprise that the recent attempt to introduce 'impact measures' for public library services in England have actually fallen back on reliance on aggregated output indicators, based on the assumption that 'reach' (or the proportion of the potential audience served) is the same as impact.[1]

LAWS OF IMPACT EVALUATION 12

Benchmarking should be seen as the beginning of a journey of discovery – not as an end in itself. The aim should be to learn more about your service by comparing its impact with that of others – not to secure a place in a table of merit.

11.7 Towards evidence-based working?

In her review of US university library engagement with impact evaluation, Covey (2002) concluded that:

> Creating a culture of assessment is not simply a matter of developing and deploying new measures or acquiring new skills. It means changing the mind

set and daily activity of librarians and support staff. To reap real and consistent benefits from assessments, libraries must pool their knowledge and experience, and organize assessment as a core activity integrated into the fabric of daily life.

What she is in effect calling for is a culture of evidence-based working. When we discussed evidence-based working earlier (section 1.1.6) we viewed it as part of the research environment but there are signs that evidence-informed and professionally based practice is creeping onto the agenda in libraries as well as in other work areas. What issues do we have to face in moving towards an impact-evaluation friendly environment? What can other work sectors tell us about creating the conditions for evidence-informed working?

11.7.1 Research dissemination and encouraging uptake

In most countries the infrastructure required to disseminate research findings across libraries and information services is generally weak. There is probably only a slight chance of library service managers knowing about any research findings and implications relating to their current preoccupations. If they decide to look for evidence, there may be no immediately obvious source that will bring together the key research findings. If they find relevant evidence, how well are they equipped to interpret findings appropriately? The same is true in other sectors. For instance, although there is a lot of work being done on making research information available in the health field, key health service workers (including hospital consultants) still need help in learning how to look for and interpret research evidence. Most other sectors, such as education and social care, still have a long way to go on making research findings available effectively.

11.7.2 Debating the nature and basis of professional knowledge and practice

This is the issue that matters. Efforts to apply evidence-based approaches to social care and education, as well as to the public health end of the health service continuum, have raised questions about the nature of professional practice and knowledge:

- Advocates of evidence-based working tend to assume that professional practice follows a technical-rational model (emphasising rules, laws, routines and prescriptions; efficient systems; technical expertise; fixed standards, knowledge seen as graspable and permanent, etc.).
- The role of professional judgement may be undervalued.
- Views of good practice arising from experience and peer discussion also tend to be discounted. This raises a real issue about what constitutes the evidence base.

Uncertainty, messiness, unpredictability and unique situations are part of the working life of most professionals. In such circumstances 'wise judgement under conditions of considerable uncertainty' is the best response available. Evidence-based working makes no allowance for this dimension. For these reasons, we prefer to advocate evidence-informed and professionally based practice. (Our colleague Andrew Booth prefers 'evidence-based and professionally informed', which opens up a further area of debate.)

11.8 Other visions

What changes will the next few years bring? Here are some possible scenarios:

- Advances in the application of information technologies, coupled with political and corporate decisions about the relative merits of libraries and other services, will lead to the demise of libraries.
- Libraries will survive by adapting to increasingly rapid changes and continually demonstrating their effectiveness.
- Libraries will play a pivotal part in the 'Age of Information' by developing and adapting services to match our increasing understanding of information literacy, how people learn and the differentiated information seeking and use behaviour of all major service user groups. This will depend upon researchers who work in such areas as information retrieval and 'information seeking in context' making common cause with library service managers to apply research knowledge in practice. (For a review of some of the potentially fertile areas of application see Kuhlthau, 2005.) In this vision of the future, some specialist libraries will evolve by moving from use of the present simplistic information retrieval systems to engagement with semantic management of information resources.

And how is the world of impact evaluation likely to change? We conclude by offering one version of the present and immediate future – even though it was written nearly two decades ago!

> The evaluation agenda has expanded . . . from an initial focus on student learning outcomes to the study of cases . . . as a better way of understanding the problems and effects of change. Evaluators have become the storytellers and theorists of innovation. . . . Evaluation is an interrogative activity intended to yield useful knowledge about social action.
>
> (Kushner and MacDonald, 1987)

Does this offer a future for library service managers as the storytellers and practitioners of innovation? We hope so.

Note

1   www.mla.gov.uk/action/framework/framework_04a.asp

References

Arnold, R. (1998) *Target Setting: school and LEA in partnership*, Slough, Education Management Information Exchange, National Foundation for Educational Research.

Babchuk, W. A. (1996) Glaser or Strauss? Grounded theory and adult education. Midwest Research-to-Practice Conference, Michigan State University, October 1997 [Winning graduate student research paper from the 1996 conference], www.anrecs.msu.edu/research/gradpr96.htm.

Baumbach, D. J. (2004) *Making the Grade: the status of school library media centers in the Sunshine State and how they contribute to student achievement*, Salt Lake City, UT, Hi Willow Research and Publishing.

Beem, C. (1999) *The Necessity of Politics: reclaiming American public life*, Chicago, University of Chicago Press.

Bell, J. (2005) *Doing Your Research Project: a guide for first-time researchers in education and social science*, Buckingham, Open University Press.

Booth, A. (2002) From EBM to EBL: two steps forward or one step back?, *Medical Reference Services Quarterly*, **21** (3), 51–64.

Booth, A. and Brice, A. (2004) *Evidence-based Practice for Information Professionals: a handbook*, London, Facet Publishing.

Brenner, M., Brown, J. and Canter, D.V. (eds) (1985) *The Research Interview: uses and approaches*, London, Academic Press.

Brice, A. and Booth, A. (2004) Consider the Evidence, *Update*, **3** (6), (June), 32.

Brigham, C. (1999) *EFQM Excellence Model*, London, Improvement and Development Agency.

Brophy, P. (2002) The Evaluation of Public Library Online Services: measuring impact, The People's Network 2002 Workshop series Issues Paper no.1, www.mla.gov.uk/documents/pn_impact.

Brophy, P. and Craven, J. (2004) Longitude II: a library networking impact toolkit for a user-driven environment, London, Museums, Libraries and Archives Council, www.mla.gov.uk/action/pn/longitude.asp.

Bundy, A. (2003a) Best Investment: the modern public library as social capital. Paper presented at the AGM of Friends of Libraries of Australia, Altona, Victoria, 27 August.

Bundy, A. (2003b) Vision, Mission, Trumpets: public libraries as social capital.
    Paper presented to NSW Country Public Libraries Association Conference
    Public Libraries Light Up Lives, Tweed Heads, NSW, 3 July,
    www.lgs.sa.gov.au/webdata/resources/Files/Conference_Paper_on_libraries_in
    _Australia/.
Burgin, R. and Bracy, P. B. (2004) *An Essential Connection: how quality school
    library media programs improve student achievement in North Carolina*, Salt
    Lake City, UT, Hi Willow Research and Publishing.
Burrows, J. and Berardinelli, P. (2003) Systematic Performance Improvement:
    refining the space between learning and results, *Journal of Workplace
    Learning*, **15** (1), 6–13.
Caplan, N., Morrison, A. and Stambaugh, R. (1975) *The Use of Social Science
    Knowledge in Policy Decisions at the National Level*, Ann Arbor, Institute of
    Social Research, University of Michigan.
Carr, E. H. (1961) *What is History?*, Harmondsworth, Middx, Penguin.
Chamberlain, D. (2003) A Pilot Study of the Use of Inter-library Loans by Clinical
    Staff, *Health Information and Libraries Journal*, **20** (4), (December), 235–9.
Cohen, D. and Prusak, L. (2001) *In Good Company: how social capital makes
    organizations work*, Boston, MA, Harvard Business School Press.
Covey, D. T. (2002) Academic library assessment: new duties and dilemmas, *New
    Library World*, **103** (1175/1176), 156–64.
Eraut, M. (2004) Practice-based Evidence. In Thomas, G. and Pring, R. (eds) q.v.,
    91–101.
Fisher, K. E., Erdelez, S. and McKechnie, E. F. (forthcoming) *Theories of
    Information Behaviour: a researcher's guide*, Medford, NJ, Information Today.
Fitz-Gibbon, C. T. (1996) *Monitoring Education: indicators, quality and
    effectiveness*, London, Cassell.
Fitz-Gibbon, C. T. and Kochan, S. (2000) School Effectiveness and Education
    Indicators. In Teddlie, C. and Reynolds, D. (eds) *The International Handbook
    of School Effectiveness Research*, London, Falmer Press.
Fullan, M. (2001) *The New Meaning of Educational Change*, 3rd edn, London,
    Cassell; New York, Teachers College Press.
Glaser, B. G. (1992) *Basics of Grounded Theory Analysis*, Mill Valley, CA,
    Sociology Press.
Glaser, B. G. and Strauss, A. L. (1967) *The Discovery of Grounded Theory:
    strategies for qualitative research*, Chicago, Aldine.
Goodhart, C. (1983) *Monetary Theory and Practice: the UK experience*, London,
    Macmillan, 96.
Gorman, G. E. and Clayton, P. (2004) *Qualitative Research for the Information
    Professional: a practical handbook*, 2nd edn, London, Facet Publishing.
Goulding, A. (2004) Libraries and Social Capital. In *Journal of Librarianship and
    Information Science*, **36** (1), 3–6.

Gray, J. and Wilcox, B. (1995) *'Good School, Bad School': evaluating performance and encouraging improvement*, Buckingham, Open University Press.

Harada, V. M. (2005) Librarians and Teachers as Research Partners: reshaping practice based on assessment and reflection. In *School Libraries Worldwide*, **11** (2), (July), 49–72.

Helm, P. (2003) Using VLEs to respond to student growth: case study on information skills development with large cohorts. Conference presentation at Umbrella 2003 'Information in Action', Chartered Institute of Library and Information Professionals, Manchester, England, 3–5 July, www.umbrella2003.org.uk/.

Holt, G. and Elliott, D. (1998) Proving Your Library's Worth: a test case, *Library Journal*, **123** (18), (November), 42–4.

Holt, G. et al. (1996) A Framework for Evaluating Public Investment in Urban Libraries, *Bottom Line*, **9** (4), (Summer), 4–13. Feature article in a special issue.

Holt, G. et al. (2001) *Public Library Benefits Valuation Study: final report to the Institute of Museums and Library services 1998–2000*, St Louis, MO, St Louis Public Library.

Hoskin, K. (1996) The 'Awful Idea of Accountability': inscribing people into the measurement of objects. In Munro, R. and Mouritsen, J., *Accountability: power, ethos and the technologies of managing*, London, International Thomson Business Press.

House, E. R. (2004) Democracy and Evaluation. Paper presented at the 6th EES Biennial Conference 2004, www.europeanevaluation.org/conferences.

Kaplan, R. S. and Norton, D. P. (1992) The Balanced Scorecard: measures that drive performance, *Harvard Business Review*, (Jan–Feb).

Kaplan, R. S. and Norton, D. P. (1993) Putting the Balanced Scorecard to Work, *Harvard Business Review*, Sept–Oct. [Both articles reprinted in *Harvard Business Review on measuring corporate performance*, Boston, USA Harvard Business School Press, 1998.]

Kinnell, M., Usherwood, R. and Jones, K. (1999a) *Improving Library and Information Services Through Self-assessment: a guide for senior managers and staff developers*, BLR+I Report 172, London, Library Association Publishing.

Kinnell, M., Usherwood, R. and Jones, K. (1999b) *The Library and Information Services Self-assessment Training Pack*, BLR+I Report 172, London, Library Association Publishing.

Knight, P. (2003) *Reducing Uncertainty*, Discussion Paper no. 4, York, Higher Education Academy.

Kuhlthau, C. C. (2005) Towards Collaboration Between Information Seeking Research and Information Retrieval, *Information Research*, **10** (2), (January), Paper 226, http://InformationR.net/ir/10-2/paper226.htm.

Kushner, S. and Macdonald, B. (1987) The Limitations of Programme Evaluation. In Murphy, R. and Torrance, H. (eds), *Evaluating Education: issues and methods*, London, Harper and Row.

Lance, K. C. and Loertscher, D. V. (2002) *Powering Achievement: school library media programs make a difference: the evidence mounts*, 2nd edn, San Jose, CA, Hi Willow Research and Publishing.

Lance, K. C. et al. (2001) *Counting on Results: new tools for outcome-based evaluation of public libraries*, Aurora, CO, Bibliographical Center for Research, www.irs.org/CoR.asp.

Lance, K. C., Welborn, L. and Hamilton-Pennell, C. (1993) *The Impact of School Library Media Centers on Achievement*, Castle Rock, CO, Hi Willow Research and Publishing.

Linley, R. and Usherwood, R. C. (1998) *New Measures for the New Library*, British Library Research and Innovation Centre Report 89, Sheffield, Centre for the Public Library in the Information Society, University of Sheffield.

Loertscher, D. V. with Todd, R. J. (2003) *We Boost Achievement! Evidence-based Practice for School Library Media Specialists*, Salt Lake City, UT, Hi Willow Research and Publishing. *Project Achievement* was based on the work published here.

Lonsdale, M. (2003) *Impact of School Libraries on Student Achievement: a review of the research report for the Australian School Library Association*, Victoria, Australian Council for Educational Research.

MacBeth, J. et al. (2001) *The Impact of Study Support*, Research Report 273, London, Department for Education and Skills.

McCarthy, A. (1999) Unpublished presentation at Library Association Executive Briefing.

McKernan, J. (1991) *Curriculum Action Research: a handbook of methods and resources for the reflective practitioner*, London, Kogan Page.

Markless, S. (2003) The Case for Action Research. In Lea, J., Hayes, D., Armitage, A., Lomas, L. and Markless, S. (2003), *Working in Post-compulsory Education*, Maidenhead, Open University Press, 146–52.

Markless, S. and Streatfield, D. R. (2000) *The Really Effective College Library*, Library and Information Commission Research Report 51, Twickenham, Middx, Information Management Associates for the Library and Information Commission [Phase 2 project report].

Markless, S. and Streatfield, D. R. (2004) *Improve your Library: a self-evaluation process for secondary school libraries and learning resource centres*, 2 vols, London, Department for Education and Skills, www.teachernet.gov.uk/schoollibraries.

Markless, S. and Streatfield, D. R. (2005) Facilitating the Impact Implementation Programme, *Library and Information Research*, **29** (91), (Spring), 10–19. The whole of this special issue of LIRN is devoted to the Impact Implementation Programme.

Markless, S. and Streatfield, D. R. (2006) Gathering and Applying Evidence of the Impact of UK University Libraries on Student Learning and Research: a facilitated action research approach, *International Journal of Information Management* (forthcoming).

Mintzberg, H. (1973) *The Nature of Managerial Work*, New York, Harper and Row [and subsequent editions].

Moore, N. (2006) *How to Do Research: the complete guide to designing and managing research projects*, 3rd rev. edn, London, Facet Publishing.

Muir Gray, J. (1997) *Evidence-based Health Care: how to make health policy and management decisions*, New York, Churchill Livingstone.

Murray, D. (2003) Whom Do You Serve?, *CILIP Update*, **2** (2), (February), 23.

O'Connor, P. (2002) Determining the Impact of Health Library Services on Patient Care: a review of the literature, *Health Information and Libraries Journal*, **19**, 1–13.

O'Neill, O. (2002) Called to Account. In *A Question of Trust: 2002 BBC Reith Lectures*, Cambridge, Cambridge University Press.

Orna, E. with Stevens, G. (1995) *Managing Information for Research*, Buckingham, Open University Press.

Parasuraman, A., Zeithaml, V. A. and Berry, L. L. (1988) SERVQUAL: a multiple-item scale for measuring consumer perceptions of service quality, *Journal of Retailing*, **64** (1), 12–40.

Parker, S. et al. (2002) *Neighbourhood Renewal and Social Inclusion: the role of museums, archives and libraries*, London, Resource, www.mla.gov.uk/documents/neighbourhood.pdf.

Parlett, M. and Dearden, G. (eds) (1977) *Introduction to Illuminative Evaluation: studies in higher education*, Cardiff-by-the-Sea, CA, Pacific Soundings Press, and Guildford, Society for Research into Higher Education.

Parlett, M. and Hamilton, D. (1972) Evaluation as Illumination: a new approach to the study of innovatory programmes; republished in Parlett, M. and Dearden, G. (eds) (1977) *Introduction to Illuminative Evaluation: studies in higher education*, Cardiff-by-the-Sea, CA, Pacific Soundings Press, and Guildford, Society for Research into Higher Education.

Popper, K. R. (1969) *Conjectures and Refutations: the growth of scientific knowledge* [new edition London, Routledge 2002].

Porter, M. E. (1985) *Competitive Advantage: creating and sustaining superior performance*, New York, Free Press.

Powell, R. R. and Connaway, L. S. (2004) *Basic Research Methods for Librarians*, 4th edn, Portsmouth, NH, Libraries Unlimited.

PriceWaterhouseCoopers (2005) *Laser Foundation: Libraries Impact Project*, London, PriceWaterhouseCoopers, www.bl.uk/about/cooperation/pdf/laserfinal6.pdf.

Putnam, R. D. (2000) *Bowling Alone: the collapse and revival of American community*, New York, Simon and Schuster.

QMW (1999) *Achieving Effective Performance Management and Benchmarking in the Public Sector*, Queen Mary Public Policy Seminars, University of London, 14th October.

Race, P. (2005) *Making Learning Happen*, London, Sage.

Reason, P. and Rowan, J. (eds) (1981) *Human Inquiry: a sourcebook of new paradigm research*, London, Wiley.

Robinson, S. and Pidd, M. (1998) Provider and Customer Expectations of Successful Simulation Projects, *Journal of the Operational Research Society*, **49** (3), 200–9.

[Scholastic] Research Foundation (2004) *School Libraries Work!*, Research Foundation Paper Danbury, CT, Scholastic Library Publishing, www.scholastic.com/grolierdocs/home.html.

Sharp, C. et al. (1999) *Playing for Success: an evaluation of the first year*, London, Department for Education and Employment.

Sharp, C. et al. (2000) *Playing for Success: an evaluation of the second year*, London, Department for Education and Skills.

Smith, M. K. (2001) Social Capital. In the *Encyclopedia of Informal Education*, www.infed.org/biblio/social_capital.htm.

Spectrum Strategy Consultants and Indepen Consulting (2004) *Measuring Our Value: results of an independent economic impact study*, London, British Library, www.bl.uk.

Strathern, M. (1997) Improving Ratings: audit in the British university system, *European Review*, **5**, 305–21.

Streatfield, D. R. (2003) *Evidence-based Museums, Archives and Libraries Work: discussion document prepared for Resource: the Council for Museums, Libraries and Archives by Information Management Associates*, Twickenham, Middx, IMA.

Streatfield, D. R. and Markless, S. (1994) *Invisible Learning? The contribution of school libraries to teaching and learning*, Library and Information Research Report 98, London, British Library Research and Development Department.

Streatfield, D. R. and Markless, S. (1997) *The Effective College Library*, British Library Research and Innovation Report 21, Developing FE Series 1 (8). London, Further Education Development Agency, [Phase 1 project report].

Streatfield, D. R. and Markless, S. (2002a) *Critical Evaluation of the LIC Value and Impact Programme: report to Resource: the Council for Museums, Libraries and Archives*, London, Resource.

Streatfield, D. R. and Markless, S. (2002b) *Review of the Benefits of Library Use in Schools, briefing paper prepared for the Department for Education and Skills*, Twickenham, Information Management Associates.

Streatfield, D. R. and Markless, S. (2003) Gathering Evidence of What We Do, *School Libraries in View*, **18** (Summer), 8–10.

Streatfield, D. R. and Markless, S. (2004) *Improve your Library: a self-evaluation process for primary schools*, London, Department for Education and Skills, www.teachernet.gov.uk/schoollibraries.

Streatfield, D. R. et al. (2000) *Rediscovering Reading: public libraries and the National Year of Reading* (with Library and Information Commission), Research Report 30, Twickenham, Middx, IMA for the LIC.

Swinbourne, K. (2000) *A Safe Place to Go: libraries and social capital*, Sydney, State Library of New South Wales Appendix 1, www.sl.nsw.gov.au/pls/publications/pdf/safe_place.pdf.

Thomas, G. (2004) Introduction: evidence and practice. In Thomas, G. and Pring, R. (eds), *Evidence-based Practice in Education*, Maidenhead, Open University Press, McGraw-Hill Education.

Thomas, G. and Pring, R. (eds) (2004) *Evidence-based Practice in Education*, Maidenhead, Open University Press, McGraw-Hill Education.

Todd, R. J. (2001) Presentation to the International Association of School Librarianship Conference.

Todd, R. J. and Kuhlthau, C. C. (2005) Student Learning Through Ohio School Libraries, part 1. How effective school libraries help students, *School Libraries Worldwide*, 11 (1), 63–88. This special issue of the International Association of School Librarianship journal is devoted to the Ohio Project.

Usherwood, R. C., Evans, M. and Jones, K. (1999) *Assessment Tools for Quality Management in Public Libraries*, BLR+I Report 155, Sheffield, Centre for the Public Library in the Information Society, University of Sheffield.

Wavell, C., Baxter, G., Johnson, I. and Williams, D. (2002) *Impact Evaluation of Museums, Archives and Libraries: available evidence project*, Prepared by the School of Information and Media, Faculty of Management, Robert Gordon University, London, Resource, www.mla.gov.uk/documents/id16rep.doc.

Webber, S. (2003) Report of the SPRIG Seminar on Information Literacy in Sport, Leisure and Tourism, Information Literacy Weblog, http://ciquest.shef.ac.uk/infolit/.

Weightman, A. L. and Williamson, J. (2005) The Value and Impact of Information Provided through Library Services for Patient Care: a systematic review, *Health Information and Libraries Journal*, 22 (1), (March), 4–25. [Work conducted on behalf of the Library and Knowledge Development Network (LKDN), Quality and Statistics Group].

Whelan, D. (2004) 13,000 Kids Can't be Wrong, *School Library Journal*, (January).

Williams, D. and Wavell, C. (2001) *The Impact of the School Library Resource Centre on Learning*, Library and Information Commission Research Report 112, Aberdeen, Faculty of Management, Robert Gordon University.

Williams, D., Wavell, C. and Coles, L. (2001) *Impact of School Library Services on Achievement and Learning: critical literature review*, London, DfES and Resource.

Williams, D., Coles, L. and Wavell, C. (2002) *Impact of School Library Services on Achievement and Learning in Primary Schools: critical literature review*, London, DfES and Resource.

Williams, D. A. et al. (2005) Implementing Impact Evaluation in Professional Practice: a study of support needs within the museum, archive and library sector, *International Journal of Information Management*, **25** (6), 533–48.

Woodcock, B. (1998) *Measuring Up: an introduction to theories and concepts of performance in public services*, London, CIPFA.

World Bank (1999) *What is Social Capital?*, www.worldbank.org/WBSITE/ EXTERNAL/TOPICS/EXTSOCIALCAPITAL.

Yin, R. K. (2002) *Case Study Research: design and methods*, 3rd edn, London, Sage.

Index

3m